# Christian
# Ethics

# Christian
# Ethics

Scripture quotations, unless otherwise noted, are from the New American Standard Bible, © The Lockman Foundation 1960, 1962, 1963, 1971, 1972, 1973, 1975, 1977. Used by permission.

Scripture quotations marked NIV are taken from The HOLY BIBLE, NEW INTERNATIONAL VERSION®. Copyright © 1973, 1978, 1984 by International Bible Society. Used by permission of Zondervan Publishing House. All rights reserved. The "NIV" and "New International Version" trademarks are registered in the United States Patent and Trademark Office by International Bible Society. Use of either trademark requires the permission of International Bible Society.

Cover design: Urban Ministries, Calumet City, IL

Interior design and typesetting: Larry Taylor Design, Ltd.

---

ISBN: 0-910566-79-8

---

7 6 5 4 3 2 1 3 2 1 0 9

# Contents

# Contents

# Ethics:
## An Introduction
## 1

In modern culture the terms *ethics* and *morals* are virtual synonyms. Quite frankly the confusion over the interchangeableness of these two terms is understandable. But it is wrong. From history we learn that the two words have different meanings. *Ethics* comes from the Greek word *ethos,* meaning a "stall" for horses, a place of stability and permanence. The word *morality* came from *mores,* which describes the shifting behavioral patterns of society.

Ethics is what is normative, absolute. It refers to a set of standards around which we organize our lives and from which we define our duties and obligations. It results in a set of imperatives that establishes behavior patterns that are acceptable. It is what people *ought* to do. By contrast, morality is more concerned with what people *do.* It describes what people are already doing, often regardless of any absolute set of standards.[1]

We now see the problem of the modern human condition. When ethics and morality are confused and mixed, the result is that the culture makes the norms. The "standards" become relativistic and changing. That which is the norm is identified with that which is the absolute. The absolute standards are consumed by the fluid nature of the culture. Relativism triumphs over the absolute.

This is where modern culture is today. We determine the norm of human behavior through statistical studies, like the Kinsey report did on human sexuality. Behavior which the Bible condemns (e.g., adultery, homosexuality) is practiced widely, statistical analysis demonstrates. Therefore, since this behavior is widely practiced, that becomes society's norm and therefore its ethical standard. Ethics becomes a relativistic, floating set of patterns which determines our duty and obligation. Nothing is absolute and nothing is forever. That which the culture thought was nailed down is not. It is as fluid as a changing river.

The Bible will have none of this. The deep-seated conviction of the Christian is the proposition that God exists and that He has revealed Himself. That revelation is verbal and propositional; it is contained in the Bible. That revelation contains the absolute set of standards rooted in God's character and will. He knows what is best for us because He created us and He redeemed us. Therefore,

His verbal revelation contains the absolute standard on which we base our lives and construct our duties and obligations to the family, the church, and the state.

To God, ethics is not a set of fluid standards. It is a set of absolutes that reflects His character and defines human duty. He wants us to love Him and love our neighbor as ourselves. This twin injunction is a powerful example of duty to God and duty to other humans. They are imperatives for all humans. They constitute a supernatural window into what is good, right, just, and perfect. As Erwin Lutzer has argued, "We must be willing to set aside temporarily the question of what actions *are* right or wrong to focus on a more basic question: what *makes* an action right or wrong?"[2] That is why God has the right to say to us, "Be holy for I am holy." He, the Creator, sets the standard against which we must measure all behavior.

## Why Study Ethics?

There are several reasons for the study of ethics. Each is separate, yet they overlap. The reasons I offer here are not exhaustive. Rather, they offer compelling evidence that the study of ethics is desperately needed in the church. Few Christians know how to think about major cultural issues ripping apart our society. Instead, they often sit on the side and allow non-Christians to dominate the discussion on abortion, human sexuality, the role of the state, issues of war, and the environment. Few seem ready to give a defense of the absolute standards of God's Word. This book gives Christians a starting point for thinking and acting on the basis of God's revelation. It enables believers to speak ethical truth to the culture.

The first reason for a study of ethics is that western culture has relinquished any absolute framework for thinking about ethical standards. One powerful example of this is bioethics. Medical technology is moving so fast that ethical considerations usually are subsumed by the practical. But this is not right! How should we think about the issue of using animal organs in human beings? Should we place a baboon's heart in a human being? Should we place animal tissue in humans? Should we use the cells of an anencephalic baby in a human? Should we use *in vitro* fertilization to help infertile couples have a baby? Should we clone human beings? Should we use gender selection in helping parents decide whether they want a boy or girl? All of these medical practices are being done or can be done. Does the Bible say anything about these issues? As later chapters in this book show, the Bible does speak to these questions and provides a set of standards and principles to guide humans in making these difficult decisions. Christians *must* be involved in this debate over bioethics (see chapter six).

A second reason focuses on the "slippery slope" nature of so many ethical questions. Consider the issue of abortion. In 1973, when the Supreme Court ruled a woman could have an abortion based on the implied right of privacy it said was in the United States Constitution, no one realized how powerful this doctrine would become. This implied right reframed the whole abortion issue. Now the culture no longer focuses on the rights of the baby; instead, the entire debate focuses on the rights of the woman to the total exclusion of the baby (see chapter four).

That same logic now informs the euthanasia debate. The discussion focuses on the right of the person to die with dignity. Doctor-assisted suicide is now sanctioned in some states using the implied right of privacy which formerly sanctioned the practice of abortion. A person who is ill and no longer desires to live, based on the implied right of privacy, can receive assistance from a doctor to commit suicide (see chapter five).

Ethical issues feed on one another. The logic of one is used by the culture to frame the debate on the other. Christians must understand this process or they will have no impact on the debates about life currently raging in our culture. The slippery slope nature of ethics without divine revelation explains why what was once unthinkable becomes debatable, and soon becomes culturally acceptable. We must come to terms with the slippery slope nature of humanistic ethics.

Third, Christians must understand the integrated nature of ethical issues. Most Christians do not know how to use the Bible to approach contemporary ethical issues. For many the Bible seems irrelevant. But this sad state of affairs cannot continue. Christians must learn to think biblically and Christianly about ethical concerns.

The Bible is God's Word. In 2 Timothy Paul argues that the Bible equips for every good work and is beneficial for correction, rebuking, and training in righteousness (3:16-17). Obviously, studying the Word is necessary for ethical decision making. God's Word gives God's view of life and His absolute standards. One cannot assume that the baby growing in the mother's womb has no value to God. If He is the Creator, as the Bible declares Him, then life is of infinite value to Him. Humans, regardless of any discussion of rights, do not have permission to wantonly destroy life. To do so violates one of God's absolute standards rooted in His character. This process of discerning God's mind on an issue, developing a principle from it, and then reaching an ethical position, is the process defended in this book. The Bible is not irrelevant toward ethics. Instead, it is the core for ethics.

Fourth, many Christians know where they stand on certain ethical issues, but they cannot defend why. This book charts a biblical defense for each position presented. For example, most Christians believe that homosexuality is wrong.

That is an ethical judgment. But why is it wrong? It is not much help to simply state, "The Bible says it is wrong." Perhaps a better defense is to root the ethical belief about human sexuality in the Creation Ordinance of God.

God created humanity in two grand streams—male and female. In Genesis 2, He makes clear that His design is that the male and female marry and "become one flesh." This solves the challenge of human loneliness and isolation that Adam experienced. Eve, as God's gift to the man, serves as his spiritual equal (both are His image, Genesis 1:26-27) but yet his complement. This complementary relationship defines the basis of human sexuality, for men and women rule the creation as God's stewards and populate His planet. Human sexuality relates to the essence of human responsibility—ruling God's creation together as a complementary whole; male and female together (Genesis 1:26ff). Whenever Jesus or Paul deals with marriage or human sexuality, each goes back to this Creation Ordinance of God (Matthew 19; 1 Corinthians 7). Here we see God's ideal for the human sexual relationship, and there is no room for homosexuality in this ordinance (see chapter seven).

Ethical decision making is a part of everyday life. Christians must not only know what they believe, they must likewise explain why. This book gives Christians a resource to define ethics as absolute standards that result in proper duty and obligation to God and fellow humans. The next chapter surveys the ethical options for Christians, defending the position of ethical absolutes as the only biblical option.

## For Further Discussion

1. Summarize the difference between *morality* and *ethics.*

2. What is the result of the confusion of ethics and morality?

3. How does God's revelation impact the view of absolute ethics?

4. List and briefly explain the four reasons for a study of ethics.

## Notes

[1] R. C. Sproul, *Ethics and the Christian* (Wheaton, IL: Tyndale House, 1986), 9-22.

[2] Erwin Lutzer, *The Necessity of Ethical Absolutes* (Dallas: Probe, 1981), 14.

# Ethical Options
# for the Christian
# 2

The thesis of this book is that a study of ethics must be rooted in the proposition that there are ethical absolutes. Those absolutes are based on God's moral law, which is revealed in His Word. Humanity can know God and understand His revelation. This claim is uniquely Christian and is central to affirming a belief in ethical absolutes. The culture's penchant for relativism is not sufficient when it comes to determining ethics because relativistic ethical systems are inadequate moral guides. Why is this so?

## Cultural Relativism

Let's examine the view of cultural relativism. This view argues that whatever a cultural group ethically approves is right and whatever the group ethically disapproves is wrong. Since there are no fixed principles to guide humans in developing ethical standards, culture determines what is right and wrong. Every culture develops its own ethical standards and, cultural relativism argues, no other culture has the right to judge another's moral standards.

Consider the consequences of cultural relativism. That there are varying cultural norms is undeniable. Whether these cultural differences ought to exist or whether all the moral viewpoints of the culture are equal must be settled by some other means. Something transcendent must reconcile these cultural differences. Furthermore, if culture determines the validity of moral behavior, we really cannot condemn any action that is acceptable within that culture. For example, from 1933–1945, Nazi Germany was acting quite consistently within its cultural worldview. Nazis believed that Jews were a threat to the perfect Aryan race they wanted to create. Therefore, to rid European civilization of Jews was logically consistent with their cultural norms. Following cultural relativism, how can Nazism be condemned?

Recent developments within higher education indicate another consequence of cultural relativism. Some students are unwilling to oppose horrific cultural practices—including human sacrifice, ethnic cleansing, and slavery—because

11

they think no one has the right to criticize the ethical standards of another group or culture. Professor Robert Simon, who has been teaching philosophy for 20 years at Hamilton College in Clinton, New York, recently indicated that his students acknowledged that the Holocaust had occurred but could not say that killing millions of people was wrong. Between 10 and 20 percent deplored what the Nazis did, but their disapproval was expressed as a matter of taste or personal preference, not one of ethical judgment. One student told Simon, "Of course I dislike the Nazis, but who is to say they were wrong?"

Another professor, Kay Haugaard of Pasadena College in California, wrote of a student in a literature class who said of human sacrifice, "I really don't know. If it was a religion of long standing...." Haugaard was stunned that her student could not make an ethical judgment: "This was a woman who wrote passionately of saving the whales, of concern for the rain forests, of her rescue and tender care of a stray dog."[1]

Cultural relativism naturally leads to individual relativism. Establishing truth in this postmodern world is relegated to the individual or the group. What is true for one is not necessarily true for another and "truths" for both groups are equally valid, for they are equally based on personal outlook. The result of this ludicrous situation reminds one of a similar situation in the book of Judges—"Every man did what was right in his own eyes" (from Judges 17:6). Individual relativism leads to social and ethical anarchy.

In the final analysis, cultural relativism propagates an unacceptable inconsistency. Denying the existence of all ethical absolutes, the system wants to proclaim its own absolute—culture![2] The argument of the ethical relativist can be summarized by three propositions:

- Since there are no universal moral standards held by all cultures, what is considered ethically right and wrong varies from culture to culture.

- Whether or not it is right for an individual to act in a certain way depends on or is relative to the culture in which he or she lives.

- Therefore, there are no absolute or objective ethical standards that apply to all people everywhere and at all times.[3]

Furthermore, the moment sin enters into the discussion, the fallacy of using culture as a basis for ethical standards is exposed. Because sin is rebellion against God, one should not expect to observe a consistency of ethical standards across various cultures. The struggle to enforce even the near-universal condemnation of murder and incest is further evidence of the human need for redemption. The problem is not culture; it is human sin! Individual or cultural relativism is not a satisfactory ethical system. In fact, it validates the need for the ethical absolutes, which are revealed in God's Word.

## Situation Ethics

One form of the ethical option called *utilitarianism* is situation ethics, which was popularized by Joseph Fletcher in his book by the same title. The core of his argument is that there really are no absolute ethical standards because over time, those standards become more important than people. The only absolute that can be affirmed is love. But how is this universal standard of love defined? For Fletcher, it must be defined in a utilitarian sense. Any action that produces more pleasure and less pain, the greatest good for the greatest number, is the "loving" thing to do. In other words, the end justifies the means.[4]

In this utilitarian understanding of "love," adultery or lying could be justified. For example, Fletcher argues that if a husband were married to an invalid, it would be loving for him to have an adulterous affair with another woman because his wife cannot meet his needs. It is likewise justifiable for a woman to have an abortion because an unwanted or unintended baby should never be born. Therefore, to abort in such situations is a loving act. But this is an indefensible ethical option: Who decides what is "loving"? Who determines the definition of the "greatest good"? We are back to a subjectivism, to an individual relativism, where each person ultimately decides his or her own definition of "good" and "loving." Situational ethics is simply a perverse variation of relativism.

## Behaviorism

A third ethical option is a product of behavioral psychology. Whether it is through genetics or the environment, humans are products of forces beyond their control, this position argues. Therefore, moral values and ethical issues are simply the product of genetic makeup or of environmental factors. The result is that one is not responsible for one's personal behavior.

One of the greatest advocates of behaviorism is the late B. F. Skinner, a famed psychologist from Harvard. Following his work with pigeons, Skinner believed he could modify the behavior of any human. In his famous book, *Beyond Freedom and Dignity,* he argued that ethical behavior is entirely based on responses to the conditioning factors of the environment. Human freedom and dignity are outmoded concepts that must be discarded if the human race is to survive. Utilizing the manipulative and conditioning techniques so central to behaviorism, Skinner maintained that "man has yet to discover what man can do for man."[5] Humanity must be willing to surrender human freedom and jettison human dignity if the race is to survive.

The Bible will have none of this. It rejects loudly the proposition that humans are not responsible for their actions (see Romans 1–3). Although a factor, environment does not totally explain human behavior. To excuse someone's actions as an exclusive product of environmental conditioning flies in the face of the biblical doctrine of sin. Humans, because they are in rebellion against God, are guilty of sin and in need of redemption. No one is ever going to stand before God and offer an acceptable behaviorist response to explain his or her sin.

## A Case for Ethical Absolutes

Theologian and pastor of the Moody Church in Chicago, Erwin Lutzer, makes this compelling argument:

> If naturalism is false and if theism is true, and therefore God is responsible for all that is, then revelation is possible. And if revelation is possible, absolute standards are possible, should the Deity choose to make them known.[6]

Has, then, God chosen "to make them known"? He has chosen to reveal Himself in His Son (Hebrews 1:1–4), through His creation (Psalm 19; Romans 1:18ff), and through His Word (Psalm 119; 2 Timothy 3:16; 2 Peter 1:21). Each is the source of propositional truth that forms the basis for ethical absolutes. Divine revelation is the basis for ethical responsibility.

What are these propositional truths that constitute the ethical framework for the Christian?

**God's moral revelation in His Word is an expression of His own nature.** As God does not change, His moral character does not change (see Malachi 3:6 and James 1:17). He is holy and therefore He insists that His human creatures also meet that standard. If they do not, judgment results. Hence, the vital nature of Jesus' substitutionary atonement. Appropriating that atoning work by faith makes the human holy and, thus, acceptable to God. The same could be argued for the ethical standards governing truth, beauty, love, life, and sexuality—each is rooted in His character.

**The moral/ethical standards and obligations that flow from His nature are absolute.** They are always binding everywhere on everyone. As Christian ethicist Norman Geisler maintains, "whatever is traceable to God's unchanging moral character is an [ethical] absolute. This includes such [ethical] obligations as holiness, justice, love, truthfulness, and mercy."[7] These ethical standards are, then, prescriptive by nature, detailing what ought to be, not what is. Culture does not provide the standard; God does in His Word.

God's moral and ethical standards consist of more than external conformity to His moral code; they also center on conformity with the internal issues of motivation and personal attitudes. Jesus' teaching of the Sermon on the Mount presses this point. The ethical standard of prohibiting adultery involves more than simply the external act; it also involves resisting the temptation to lust in the heart after another woman (Matthew 5:27-28). The ethical standard of prohibiting murder involves more than the external act; it also involves the standard of bitterness, hatred, and anger in the heart (vv. 21-22).

Because ethical standards flow from God's very nature and character, they are deontological; His ethical standards are duty-centered, not result-centered. God's ethical standards are always right to follow, even if one does not see immediate results. For example, it is always right to stand against racism, bigotry, and hatred, even if laws are not changed or human behavior remains unaltered. Jesus summarized this best when He declared that humans are to "love the Lord your God with all your heart and with all your soul and with all your mind and with all your strength....Love your neighbor as yourself" (Mark 12:30-31, NIV). He clearly defines our duty toward God and other humans.

**God provides the absolute criterion for determining the value of human beings.** Because each is arbitrary and relative, physical, economic, mental, and social or cultural criteria are all inadequate for assigning value to humans. For example, Francis Crick, the Nobel prize–winning biologist, has advocated legislation in which newborn babies would not be considered legally alive until they were two days old and had been certified as healthy by medical examiners. Senator Charles Percy, former Senator from Illinois, once argued that abortion is a good deal for the taxpayer because it is considerably cheaper than welfare. Winston L. Duke, a nuclear physicist, stated that reason, which demonstrates self-awareness, volition, and rationality, should be the criterion for assigning human value and worth. Therefore, since not all humans manifest these qualities, not all are human. Finally, Ashley Montagu, famed British anthropologist, argued that a baby is not born human. Instead, it is born with a capacity for becoming human as he or she is molded by social and cultural influences.[8]

That God created humans in His image (Genesis 1:26ff) establishes His absolute criterion for assigning value to human beings. Being in the image of God means that humans resemble God. Humans possess self-consciousness, self-will, and moral responsibility, as does God. What humans lost in the fall (Genesis 3) was righteousness, holiness, and knowledge; these are renewed in the Christian as he or she is conformed to the image of Christ. What in theology are called the communicable attributes (e.g., love, holiness, mercy, etc.) are present and possible in humans. But being made in His image also means that humans represent God.  God's purpose in creating humanity in His image is functional (see clear context of Genesis 1:26-27). Humans have dominion over God's creation; they are His stewards. This concept is emphasized in Genesis 2 and reiterated in Psalms 8 and 110. Man is God's vice-regent with the power to control, regulate, and harness creation's potential. The fall did not abolish this stewardship. Instead, Satan is the usurper and enemy of humans in this dominion status. Man lives out of harmony with himself and with nature. Created to rule, man finds that the crown has fallen from his brow. (On the image of God concept, see Anthony Hoekema, *Created in God's Image*.)

The biblical perspective on humanity is likewise defined in the Reformed concept of the "created person." According to Scripture, a human is both a creature and a person. To be a creature means absolute dependence on God; to be a person means relative independence. To be a creature means I cannot move a finger or utter a word apart from God. To be a person means that when my fingers are moved, I am the one moving them, and when words are uttered by my lips, I have uttered them. The creaturehood and the personhood of humans must be held both together and in tension. When theology stresses creaturehood and subordinates personhood, a hard-faced determinism surfaces and man is dehumanized. When personhood is stressed to the exclusion of creaturehood, man is defiled and God's sovereignty is compromised.[9]

As Francis Schaeffer has argued, "Unlike the evolutionary concept of an impersonal beginning plus time plus chance, the Bible gives an account of man's origin as a finite person made in God's image...."[10] Humans have personality, dignity, and value and are superbly unique. Unlike the naturalistic worldview, where there is no qualitative difference between humanity and other life, the Bible declares the infinite value of all humans. This proposition is the foundation for examining all ethical issues that relate to life.

## For Further Discussion

1. Define and then give a reasoned critique of the following ethical options:

   • Cultural/Ethical Relativism

   • Situation Ethics (utilitarianism)

   • Behaviorism

2. How does the proposition that God has revealed Himself relate to ethical absolutes?

3. What can we say about God's standard concerning the following?

- The external and the internal dimensions of moral/ethical behavior
- The value of human life to God
- The image of God concept
- The created person concept

4. On what basis can we say that humans are of infinite value to God? Explain.

### Notes

[1] James P. Eckman, "Preparing for the Postmodern Challenge," *Grace Tidings*, November 1997, 1.

[2] Erwin Lutzer, *The Necessity of Ethical Absolutes* (Dallas: Probe, 1981), 24.

[3] Louis P. Pojman, *Ethics: Discovering Right and Wrong* (Belmont, CA: Wadsworth, 1995), 35.

[4] See Lutzer, 24-39.

[5] B. F. Skinner, *Beyond Freedom and Dignity* (New York: Knopf, 1971), 231.

[6] Lutzer, 70.

[7] Norman Geisler, *Christian Ethics: Options and Issues* (Grand Rapids, MI: Baker, 1989), 23.

[8] Bill Crouse, *Abortion and Human Value* (Dallas: Probe, 1979), 1-4.

[9] Anthony A. Hoekema, "Created Persons," *The Reformed Journal*, March 1986, 9.

[10] Francis Schaeffer and C. Everett Koop, *Whatever Happened to the Human Race?* (Old Tappan, NJ: Revell, 1979), 153.

# How Should a Christian Relate to Culture?

## 3

The Bible warns against "worldliness" and the devastating consequences of following the world and not Christ (James 4). From the Old Testament we see that the children of Israel got into big trouble when they imitated their pagan neighbors and brought their altars and images into the temple. Yet, Christians are somehow to be in the world but not of the world (John 17:14-18). Christians have been removed from the world's power at conversion (Galatians 6:14) and, because the cross established a judicial separation between believers and the world, Christians are citizens of a new kingdom (Philippians 3:20). The Bible both discourages absolute physical separation from the people of the world (1 Corinthians 5:9-10), yet instructs believers to witness to this world (John 17:18), all the while keeping from the influence of the world (James 1:27; 1 Corinthians 7:31; Romans 12:2; 1 John 2:15). How does one resolve this tension?

This is a profoundly important question for those who hold to ethical absolutes. In a culture that is increasingly pagan and relativistic, how one "speaks" Christianity to the culture is critical. Should Christians separate from the culture and live in isolation? Should Christians seek to accommodate completely to the culture and seek to influence its institutions and values from the inside? Or should Christians seek to transform the culture by seeking to control its institutions and claim each for Christ? Historical examples for each are readily available from church history and present today in our world. The goal of this chapter is to examine and biblically evaluate each model.[1]

## The Separational Model

The separational model of relating to culture argues that Christians must withdraw from any involvement in the world. There is an antithesis between the kingdom of God and the kingdom of this world and the choice is clear—withdraw. Clear biblical examples of this choice are Noah (whom God called out of the culture before He destroyed it), Abram (called to separate from pagan Mesopotamia), and Moses (called to separate from idolatrous Egypt). The New

Testament buttresses this conviction with verses like Matthew 6:24 ("No one can serve two masters..."), 1 Peter 2:11, and 1 John 2:15. For this model, the church of Jesus Christ is a counterculture that lives by kingdom principles. She is to have nothing to do with this world.

One historical example of this model centers on the church before Constantine's critical decree in A.D. 313. During this time, the church refused to serve in the Roman army, refused to participate in pagan entertainment, and refused to bow to Caesar as lord. It was antagonistic and separated from the culture, yet sought to win it to Christ.

Another historical example is Anabaptism, exemplified in the various Mennonite and Amish groups of the sixteenth century, many of whom continue today. For them there is an absolute antithesis between the kingdom of God and this world. This necessitates a rejection of the church-state concept—the revolutionary center of their worldview. The church, in their view, is a free association of believers; there is no "established" state church. Religious liberty, non-resistance, often pacifism, and refusal to take vows and oaths separate these communities from the world. Isolated and separate, social service establishes and furthers Christ's kingdom on earth.

A final historical example is the Christian community movement, growing out of the 1960s, when Christian communes dotted the American and European religious landscape. Clearly countercultural, these groups believed that the church had become hopelessly secularized. Therefore, Christianity needed to get back to the Book of Acts where resources were shared, lifestyles were simple, and believers were clearly separate from the hostile culture. This alternative way, rooted in a radical separation, would lead the church back to its roots and to revival.

How should we think about the separational model? In a culture that is increasingly pagan and antagonistic, much is appealing about Christianity. This model stresses the "other-worldly" character of a genuinely biblical Christianity and calls people to recognize that "this world is not my home," as we often sing. After all, Jesus radically rejected the status quo of His culture and died as a result. Yet, this model has serious dangers that necessitates its rejection as a viable option.

There are three dangers to this model. First, separatism can quickly lead to asceticism, a lifestyle of self-denial that ends up denying the goodness of God's creation. From God's declaration in Genesis 1 that all of His creation is "good" to Paul's powerful affirmation that everything is created by God and nothing is to be rejected (1 Timothy 4:4), the Bible condemns all tendencies toward an asceticism that denies creation's innate goodness. Second, this model easily produces a dangerous sacred/secular dichotomy. For the believer, the Bible clearly rejects the compartmentalization of life into things that are sacred and those that are secular. For the Christian, everything is sacred. Paul writes in 1 Corinthians 10:31 that the believer is to "do all to the glory of God." Finally, this model can lead to a complete withdrawal from culture, something clearly condemned in the Bible. In 1 Corinthians 5:9-11 Paul chastises the Corinthians for misunderstanding his admonition about disciplining the wayward brother. He says they processed incorrectly his teaching about not associating with sinners. The only way to do so was to die, and that is not what he wanted them to do. So, the separational model is inadequate for the believer.

## The Identificational Model

Accommodation to the culture is the key word for this model: to live both in the kingdom of God and in the world. God works in the world both through the state and through the church. The believer, therefore, has a dual commitment to both the church and the state. Identifying with, participating in, and working within all cultural institutions (e.g., business, government, law) is part of the mandate for the Christian. Christians are, therefore, to live both in the kingdom of God and the kingdom of this world.

Biblical examples of this model abound. Joseph rose to the top of ancient Egypt, serving as a sort of prime minister (Genesis 41:41-43). Similarly, Daniel played key political and advisory roles in the empires of both Babylon and Persia (Daniel 6:1-4). Jesus identified with the world, eating and drinking with tax collectors and assorted sinners. He clearly did not separate from the world, for He was a friend of Nicodemas and associated with key officials in the Roman army (e.g., the centurion). Finally, the Book of Acts records apostles associating with the Ethiopian eunuch and Cornelius, another Roman official. Paul, in Romans 13:1-7, illustrates the role of the state as a clear sphere of God's work.

Historical examples are likewise numerous. After Constantine's 313 decree, the church-state dynamic changed. He restored church property. Bishops became equal with Roman officials. Over time the church became wealthy and powerful. Christianity became popular, the "in-thing" for the empire. Complacency resulted. Its power became political and through the medieval period (A.D. 500 –1500) it gained immense prestige and dominance. In fact, during the papacy of Innocent III (early 1200s), the church in effect ruled Western Europe.

Another example is modern civil religion, which sees the nation-state as ordained by God for a special redemptive mission. For American religious leaders like Jonathan Edwards, Charles Finney, and Lyman Beecher, God chose America to be the savior of the world, a chosen people to accomplish redemptive purposes for all humanity. God's kingdom, they argued, would come first to America and then would spread through the rest of the world. Manifest Destiny, which defined American foreign policy in the pre-Civil War period, saw America's institutions as perfect and God destined that those institutions be spread through North America. Such thinking had its origins in civil religion and partially explains the Mexican-American War (1846–1848) and other forms of expansionism. Similar arguments could be made about expansionism in the late nineteenth century, specifically the Spanish-American War of 1898.

As we evaluate the identificational model, its strengths are clear. It emphasizes "this worldly" character of the Christian life. There is much in this world that can and should be affirmed because it is ultimately good. This model calls people to recognize that there is importance and good in this world now. It likewise affirms that God is at work in and through the cultural institutions like the state, business, and even the arts. A Christian can identify and find benefit in each of these institutions.

However, its weaknesses are glaring. Its principal danger is that the identificational model can lull the Christian into complacency, into a blindness toward the influence of evil in the culture's institutions. Anyone involved in politics knows that it is the greatest test of one's faith to work in politics. Evil is always present and the pressure to compromise one's convictions is ever present. This model can also lead to an uncritical acceptance of prevailing cultural practices and attitudes. Particularly in democracies where majority rule is so prevalent, pressures to go with polling data as the basis for decision-making is often tempting. The more Christians identify with the institutions, the more the institutions influence the Christian. Contemporary society is more permissive than that of the past and the evangelical community is being affected by that permissiveness.

Finally, this model can lead to a loss of the church's prophetic stance. The church can almost become "married to the culture." One disastrous example is the church in Nazi Germany. It was crying, "better Hitler than Stalin," and uncritically embraced Hitler's state as a matter of expediency. The same happened in American culture, especially to justify the Mexican-American War and aspects of the Spanish-American War. This model has the danger, then, of producing a complacent and soft Christianity.

## The Transformational Model

This model takes the transforming power of Christ and applies it to culture. Despite the fallen nature of humanity and the subsequent curse of creation, Jesus' death, burial, and resurrection reversed the curse for both humans and culture. There is now hope of human release from the bondage to sin and for creation as well. This is the center of ancient Israel's hope that the world would be restored (Isaiah 65) and of the New Testament's focus on Christ's redemptive work (Romans 5:12-21). Romans 8:19-22 also emphasizes the complete re-making of creation from sin's curse. This hope is easily translated into an optimism about culture's transformation.

Historical examples of this model center on the transforming work of the Gospel in a geographical area. During the Reformation, John Calvin's Geneva reflected this transforming power. Calvin taught the total lordship of Christ, that it extended to the state and to economics.

Therefore, the government of Geneva experienced radical reform and pursued righteousness in making and enforcing its laws. Work to Calvin and Geneva was a God-ordained vocation, whatever its specific nature. The city, therefore, experienced remarkable economic transformation as well. A similar change process characterized the Puritan colony of Massachusetts Bay in the 1600s. All aspects of the Puritan culture were brought into conformity with God's revelation. It was complete cultural transformation.

There is much to affirm in this model. It recognizes the Gospel's power to change both individuals and their culture. It is common sense to expect that when a person trusts Christ, his or her lifestyle and culture will therefore change. Ultimately, nothing is immune in culture from the Gospel's impact. Likewise, this model calls on Christians to recognize their responsibility to work toward the day when God's kingdom will come to earth and justice will rule (Amos 5:15, 24).

There are, however, several serious shortcomings with this model. The transformationist can neglect the radical nature of sin's devastation. Humans remain enslaved to sin and even believers daily struggle with its power. Scripture abounds with warnings about how subtle and powerful the enemies of the world, the flesh, and the devil really are. In addition, the transformational model can promote an unbiblical optimism, a near utopianism. The Bible rejects such optimism apart from the return of Jesus Christ. Humans, even those regenerated by faith, always struggle with sin and it will only be when Jesus returns that the victory over evil will be complete. The transformational model must therefore also be rejected.

## The Incarnational Model

Robert Webber proposes a synthesis of all three models as proper for the believer.[2] His proposal is modeled after Jesus, for He separated from the evils of His culture, identified with its institutions and people, yet sought to transform it from the inside out. By adding humanity to His deity, Jesus identified with the world its social order, i.e., its people and its customs. Similarly, the church is to do the same. At bottom, this is the heart of Christ's admonition that we are to be in the world but not of the world. Yet Christ separated Himself from the evil distortions of the created order. He had nothing to do with the distorted use of wealth, social position, or political power. Finally, through His death, burial, and resurrection, He broke the power of sin and Satan and guarantees the world's transformation when He returns in glory and power. Similarly, the church is to move culture's institutions toward genuine, biblical righteousness, all the while anticipating His final transforming work when He returns.

How does the believer live out Webber's incarnational model? First, the Christian always lives with tension, the tension between that which is transformable and that from which he or she must separate. For example, there are many good structures in the culture—art, economics, sports, vocations—yet there are always the evil distortions of those good structures—pornography, greed, workaholism, idolatry. The Christian should identify with the good structures and seek their transformation but always separate from those evil distortions. Second, there is no simple formula for living with or resolving this tension. Looking for the biblical answer to each practical question is rarely possible. Applying the principles of Scripture to each person's situation may well produce considerably different judgments. The believer's responsibility is to know God's Word, to know the mind of Christ, and then choose a course of action that each believes most faithfully represents God's revealed will.

What are some examples of this tension? In seeking to identify with the cultural structures, while separating from their evil distortions, should a Christian own a television, listen to non-Christian music, be on the Internet? Obviously, believers will answer these questions differently but how each is answered represents the variety of expressions within the Christian church. How Christians personally resolve this tension should produce a healthy biblical tolerance, a thankfulness for the multiplicity of expressions of Christianity. It is not easy to resolve the tension between identifying with the culture's institutions and structures and seeking to separate from the distortions of each. Some Christians will choose not to own a television, not to listen to secular music, and not to have an Internet connection. Agreeing to disagree on such matters guards against unhealthy legalism and promotes a healthy dialogue about living within a non-Christian culture.

Christians must always reconcile the tension of identifying with cultural institutions, seeking to separate from culture's evil distortions, all the while seeking culture's transformation. How we live with that tension is a mark of spiritual maturity.

## For Further Discussion

1. Summarize the Bible's teaching about the world and the Christian's relation to it.

2. Define the essence of each of the following models of Christians relating to culture. Give the biblical justification for each as well.

   • The separational model

   • The identificational model

   • The transformational model

3. Summarize the strengths and weaknesses of each model.

4. Robert Webber suggests a synthesis of all three models, which he calls the incarnational model. Explain what he means.

5. What does the author mean when he discusses the tension between identifying with culture's institutions and structures and yet separating from its evil distortions? What are some of the guiding principles he offers to help resolve the tension?

## Notes

[1] Robert E. Webber, *The Secular Saint: A Case for Evangelical Social Responsibility* (Grand Rapids, MI: Zondervan, 1979).

[2] Ibid.

# Abortion
## 4

The abortion crisis in American civilization has been called a modern holocaust. An exaggeration? Not if you maintain a biblical view of life. The purpose of this chapter is to review briefly the history of abortion in America, develop a biblical view of human life, and answer several salient questions germane to the issue.

### The History of Abortion in America

By a seven to two decision, in 1973 the United States Supreme Court in the case *Roe v. Wade*, handed down one of its most radical decisions in modern history. Generally, when a case reaches the Supreme Court, the Court is asked to rule on a constitutional question. The Court decides what the Constitution says, and in this case the Court was asked whether states (in this case Missouri) can restrict a women's right to abortion. The Court could not cite any specific part of the Constitution that established the right of abortion, nor could they find such a right in the Bill of Rights (the first ten amendments to the Constitution). Therefore, the Court set a precedent that did not directly appeal to the Constitution; instead, it declared that there is an implied right of privacy in the Constitution and on that basis established the right of women to have abortions. In its decision, the Court stipulated that abortions could occur up to the point of "viability" (i.e., when a child can live outside the womb) but did not define when this was. The Court further stipulated that the health of the mother must play a role in defining viability but did not define the "health of the mother" concept. The result of *Roe v. Wade* is that the United States has one of the most liberal abortion laws in the world. For all practical purposes, it is abortion on demand—abortion as a form of birth control. Whatever the specifics of the pregnancy, if a woman can find a sympathetic doctor or clinic, abortion is guaranteed.

The Court argued that the weight of history was on the side of abortion. The idea that life begins at conception is a modern idea and must be rejected, it contended. Why? Since there is no consensus in the medical community or among theologians or philosophers as to when life begins, the Court would not decide the issue either. The weight of the Court's argument really rested on the proposition that the unviable fetus derives its meaningfulness solely from the mother's desire to give birth to her baby. In other words, the mother's rights are established absolutely to the total exclusion of the baby's.

Today American society tolerates several types of abortion:

- Therapeutic abortion—when the termination of a pregnancy is necessary for the sake of the mother's health.

- Psychiatric abortion—for the sake of the mother's mental health.

- Eugenic abortion—to prevent the birth of deformed, retarded children.

- Social abortion—for economic reasons, especially as related to the financial needs of the family.

- Ethical abortion—in the cases of rape or incest.

Again, the result of such practices is a culture where abortion on demand is available to anyone desiring it.

Although gruesome, it is important to review the methods of abortion practiced in the United States. Each method results in the death of a living human being:

- The dilation and curettage method (D and C)—Performed early in pregnancy, in this procedure the surgeon cuts the fetus and the placenta into pieces and removes them from the womb.

- The suction method—The surgeon draws the fetus out of the womb via powerful suction tube, killing the baby.

- The saline method—During the latter weeks of the pregnancy, the surgeon injects a salt solution through the abdomen of the mother, poisoning the baby in about an hour. Twenty-four hours later, the baby is delivered stillborn.

- Chemical abortions—This is a more recent development, usually involving the administration of a drug (e.g., RU-486) to the mother which, in effect, causes the woman's body to abort a recently fertilized egg. This is the most problematic of methods because it does not involve a medical procedure, only the administration of pills.

## A Biblical View of Prenatal Life

Modern medicine affirms a proposition that is quite consistent with God's Word—life is a continuum. (For the Christian, life extends from conception on into eternity, for all human beings will live forever.) The DNA strands present at conception are species-specific and the beginning of a new and unique individual human. Indeed, Keith L. Moore and T. V. N. Persaud, in a major medical textbook, *Developing Human*, argue that

> Human development begins at fertilization, the process during which a male... sperm unites with a female [egg] to from a single cell called a zygote. This highly specialized, totipotent cell marked the beginning of each of us as a unique individual. [A zygote is defined] as the beginning of a new human being. Although most developmental changes occur during the embryonic and fetal periods, some important changes occur during later periods of development: infancy childhood, adolescence, and adulthood. Although it is customary to divide human development into *prenatal* (before birth) and *postnatal* (after birth) periods, birth is merely a dramatic event during development resulting in a change in environment.[1]

But unfortunately, in 1973 the Supreme Court was right: There was no consensus in the culture about when life begins. God's revelation in the Bible, however, has spoken to this issue. A thorough examination of His Word reveals that God views life in the womb as of infinite value and in need of protection. The challenge is that most areas of the culture—law, politics, many theologians and religious leaders—refuse to heed God's clear teaching on this issue of prenatal life.

A cluster of verses in the Bible clearly establishes God's view of prenatal life:

- Luke 1:41, 44; 2:12, 16; Exodus 21:22—Unborn babies are called "baby" or "child," the same word used of infants and young children.

- Matthew 1:20-21; Luke 1:26-27—Jesus Christ was fully human (the God-man), which included His conception in the womb of Mary. Unequivocally, from God's perspective, the embryo in Mary's womb was Jesus and was of infinite worth and value.

- Exodus 21:22-24—Whatever these difficult verses exactly mean, God views life in the womb as of great value. Whether by accident or by intent, to cause a woman to miscarry demands accountability on the part of the one who caused it. The law did not treat the fetus frivolously.

- Isaiah 49:1, 5—Referring to Messiah, God called Him for His mission from the womb. Life that is prenatal is precious to God.

- Jeremiah 1:5; Luke 1:15—As with Isaiah, God viewed Jeremiah and John the Baptist from the womb as of infinite value. He even filled John with the Holy Spirit when he was in Elizabeth's womb.

No other passage deals with the question of prenatal life so powerfully and conclusively as does Psalm 139. In this wonderful psalm, David reviews four phenomenal attributes of God—His omniscience, His omnipresence, His omnipotence, and His holiness. In reviewing God's omnipotence, David summarizes God's power in creating life, which he compares to God "weaving" him in his mother's womb. God made his "frame," his skeleton. Then, in verse 16, he writes, "Your eyes have seen my *unformed substance*" (emphasis added). Undoubtedly, David is referring to the embryo. Even before his mother knew she was pregnant, God knew David and was intimately involved in all aspects of his development. He even declares that God, in effect, planned his entire life—from his beginning. The divine perspective on life is that it begins at conception. So awesome is God's omniscience and His omnipotence, that He knew all about David even when he was an embryo! This is God's view of life. This is God's judgment on abortion. The intentional taking of an unborn baby's life is, therefore, homicide.

## Ethical Questions Relating to Abortion

**Is the fetus a human being?** At conception, all aspects of humanness, as defined by DNA, are present. Genetically, it is quite difficult to argue otherwise. The above biblical passages also declare quite forcefully that God views the fetus as a human being.

**Is the human fetus a person?** Quite frankly, the pro-abortion position is categorical: The unborn child is not a person. Indeed, even in the *Roe v. Wade* decision, the Supreme Court argued that if the right of personhood is established, the "appellant's case [the pro abortion position], of course, collapses, for the fetus' right to life is then guaranteed specifically by the [14th Amendment]."[2] This is, therefore, an increasingly pressing question today. In pro-abortion circles, the biological term "life" has been exchanged for the legal term "person." This is a critical switch in terms because only "persons" have rights, including the right to life. Paul and John Feinberg argue in their book, *Ethics for a Brave New World*, that at conception the DNA strands of the embryo are species-specific. Furthermore, although the fetus is dependent upon the mother, he or she is an independent individual. In addition, there is substantial identity between the embryo, the viable fetus, the infant, the child, the adult and the elderly person.[3] Life is indisputably a continuum and one cannot isolate the fetus and call it a non-person. That is both medically and theologically fallacious. The fetus is a "person."

**How do the rights of the fetus relate to the rights of the mother?** American culture has so totally focused on the rights of the mother that it gives no credence to the rights of the fetus. As this chapter has shown, this is ethically wrong. There must be a balance of rights. Christians must make the case for protecting the rights of the unborn child. Paul and John Feinberg have suggested a starting point:

> While it is difficult, and perhaps impossible, to convince a pro-abortionist of the personhood of the fetus, nevertheless from a purely ethical point of view it still makes sense to demand that human life should not be arbitrarily terminated, particularly when less dramatic solutions exist. Such solutions should be sought on the side of both the fetus and the mother. Having once been conceived, the fetus has no choice but to grow, just as it had no choice in its conception or its blond hair or blue eyes. Hence, the fetus is without recourse or remedy. The same is not true of the mother, who has at least three alternatives other than abortion. She can exercise initial will power by abstinence, which is grossly out of fashion today. She has the option to use contraceptives to prevent the unwanted child. And finally, given the birth of the child, the mother can allow the living but unwanted infant to be put up for adoption.[4]

Abortion is, therefore, an unacceptable practice from God's viewpoint. He views prenatal life as of infinite worth and value. To wantonly destroy it is to destroy that which He views as precious. American society may have the legal right to enforce abortion (following *Roe v. Wade*), but it does not have the ethical right before God to do so. Is it a modern holocaust? With nearly 50 million abortions since 1973, it is difficult to argue otherwise.

**What about contraception?** The introduction of the birth control pill in the 1950s, and the financial and legal support of the pill from the federal government, moved contraceptives from being illegal to being the norm for most of 21st-century humanity. As culture has accommodated itself to the norm of contraception, an effective separation of sex and procreation has occurred and the cultural consequences are hardly positive. Sexual activity now occurs without any concern for pregnancy, such that procreation is one of the least important aspects of marriage and sex. There is little doubt that the contraceptive revolution has played a major role in the moral decline of Western civilization. Hence, contraception is an ethical issue.

As we consider the ethics of contraceptive medications, the perplexing nature of this issue is enhanced when one understands that some of the medications exclusively prevent fertilization and some hinder the implantation of the week-old embryo in the uterine wall of the mother. For example, RU-486 (Mifepristone) blocks a hormone required to sustain a pregnancy, which is then accompanied by another pill (Misoprostol), which induces contractions and expels the fetus from the mother's body. Also, there are "emergency contraceptive pills," which involve estrogens, progestins, and other hormones that prevent ovulation or fertilization, and some that prevent the implantation of the embryo in the uterine wall. Finally, Plan B is a brand of hormones promoted by Planned Parenthood and others as a "morning-after pill." All of these are, in effect, abortifacients (i.e., cause an abortion of the embryo).

Less controversial methods of birth control include the rhythm method, which involves a couple refraining from sexual intercourse during a certain number of days when the woman is thought to be fertile. Similarly, the natural family planning method observes the physical changes in a woman's body to determine when she is ovulating and susceptible to contraception. Avoiding sexual intercourse during these days prevents a pregnancy. In addition, there are various barrier methods, including male condoms, the diaphragm, contraceptive sponges, cervical caps, and female condoms.

Finally, in terms of basic contraceptive products, there is the oral contraceptive pill (there are about forty types on the market), which are hormonal contraceptives that prevent ovulation and override the woman's normal reproductive cycle, in effect tricking the body into thinking a pregnancy has occurred. At least 10 million women in the United States and more than 100 million worldwide use this kind of contraceptive pill.

So, what do we do as Christians? Should Christians use birth control of any type? Are some acceptable and others not? Certainly, those chemical contraceptives that are, in effect, abortifacients are questionable and probably ethically unacceptable for the Christian couple. In a book this size, it is impossible to detail specific observations about the medical or ethical appropriateness of the many contraceptive products on the market. There is, therefore, a degree of biblically oriented wisdom needed on this matter. To that end, permit me to quote from Old Testament theologian Michael Grisanti of Master's Seminary:

> Any decisions we make must be compatible with recognition that God has ultimate sovereignty, and this is not an area for us to regard as a secular province under our control. God values children highly and so should we. Since the Bible does not explicitly condemn or condone birth control, we must employ biblical (rather than worldly) wisdom in determining how we as couples can best bring God great glory through this stewardship of marriage and sexual intimacy.[5]

As with all things, we must begin our thinking and then make our ethical decisions based on God's Word and the wisdom than comes from our study of His Word. May God give us that passion and that wisdom as we serve Him and represent Him, even in difficult issues such as contraception.

## For Further Discussion

1. Summarize the Supreme Court's legal argument in the 1973 decision *Roe v. Wade*. In your opinion, what did the Court ignore? Does it seem that it consulted the Bible? How would you critique it?

2. What are the types of abortion recognized in our culture today?

3. Why might pills like RU-486 be potentially problematic for those who are against abortion? Do further reading to find out how safe this pill really is.

4. Using the verses cited in this chapter, write a biblical position paper on why abortion is not in God's will. Be sure to stress Psalm 139.

5. Is the fetus a human? A person? How would you present an argument that the fetus is of great value and should be protected by U.S. law? How would you make an argument that life begins at conception?

6. Summarize some of the important ethical issues surrounding contraception.

## Notes

[1] Keith L. Moore and T. V. N. Persaud, *The Developing Human: Clinically Oriented Embryology*, 6th ed. (Philadelphia: W. B. Saunders Company, 1998), 2, 18.

[2] Norman Geisler, *Christian Ethics: Options and Issues* (Grand Rapids, MI: Baker, 1989), 136.

[3] John Feinberg and Paul Feinberg, *Ethics for a Brave New World* (Wheaton, IL: Crossway, 1993), 58ff.

[4] Feinberg and Feinberg, 71.

[5] Michael A. Grisanti, "Birth Control and the Christian: Recent Discussion and Basic Suggestions," *The Master's Seminary Journal* 23/1 (Spring 2012): 111-112. (The entire section on birth control is dependent on this valuable article.)

# Euthanasia
## 5

Like abortion, euthanasia is one of the critical life issues facing American culture today. With baby boomers growing older, the pressure for the culture to consider widespread euthanasia will grow. For example, in a very famous speech delivered in the 1980s, former governor of Colorado, Richard Lamb, argued that the elderly must die—must embrace euthanasia—to make way for the young, who simply cannot afford the medical care needed for the elderly. With the population living longer and with medical costs soaring, the pressure over the next several decades to see euthanasia as a solution will be relentless.

But this consideration of euthanasia as a viable solution is not only for the elderly. What about the incurably ill whose life is sustained only by a ventilator or some other form of medical technology? Or, consider the malformed baby or the severely retarded child who will never live a "quality life." The financial cost to society in caring for the elderly, the severely ill, or the malformed or retarded child is enormous, and that cost is growing each year. Because of the suffering, is it not reasonable to end such lives in a merciful manner? Does it not also make financial sense to do so?

Each of these examples represents people who will in all probability never live a "quality" life and quality of life seems intuitively quite important in making end-of-life decisions. Is the quality-of-life ethic a valid one? How should Christians respond? How should believers think about mercy killings, doctor-assisted suicide, "death with dignity," and heroic measures to save and sustain a person's life? How one views abortion often gives a hint as to how one views euthanasia because both focus on the value of human life. This chapter will argue that, whether human life is in a mother's womb or on a deathbed at age ninety, it is of infinite value to God: Human life bears His image.

## Euthanasia Defined

The term "euthanasia" is derived from two Greek words meaning "well" or "good" death. It is today associated with language that seeks to sanitize the reality of death. "Death with dignity" focuses on constitutionally establishing the right of humans to die in a manner they choose. Usually, the reference point is old age when the bodily systems are beginning to shut down, but it can actually apply to anyone who is dying or extremely ill with a fatal disease. "Mercy killing" refers to taking a person's life or allowing him to take his own life to end the suffering that goes with a particular disease or a specific physical ailment or condition. Finally, "doctor-assisted suicide" refers to doctors providing one of a variety of means so that an individual can, in effect, end his or her life. That "assistance" from a doctor might involve a prescription, an injection, or some other procedure that empowers the individual, not the doctor, to end life.

The concept of euthanasia, likewise, involves several types or methods used to effect the death. "Voluntary or involuntary euthanasia" defines whether the patient requests or has taken an active role in deciding upon the death. "Active or passive euthanasia" determines the method used to bring about the death. "Passive" euthanasia would involve, for example, allowing the natural means of the body to bring death without any intervention. Not hooking a patient up to a ventilator or a heart machine would be examples because death would most certainly follow. "Active" euthanasia focuses on a loved one actively taking the person's life with a weapon or removing the life-sustaining equipment from the patient, thereby bringing on death. "Direct or indirect" euthanasia stresses the role of the patient who dies from a specific action. Doctor-assisted suicide, where a medical doctor gives a patient the equipment or medicine to end life, would be an example of direct euthanasia. The late Dr. Jack Kevorkian of Michigan promoted this type of euthanasia.

Another example is the retired anesthesiologist Lawrence Egbert, who is in some ways the current public face of doctor-assisted suicide in the United States. He has replaced Kevorkian as the symbol of this controversial practice. His method of assisting people who wish to end their life is what he calls the "exit hood." Connected to two helium tanks, the hood is placed over a person's head, the helium is released and within minutes the person is dead. Using this hood, typically, a person loses consciousness in thirty to sixty seconds and is dead within five to ten minutes. Egbert estimates he has been present for one hundred suicides over the past fifteen years using his method. As the medical director of Final Exit Network (created in 2004), a loosely knit group that claims three thousand dues-paying members, he has approved applications for about three hundred suicides. He has approved people who are struggling with depression as well as those suffering from cancer and other life-threatening diseases. Egbert instructs his patients where they can buy the helium tanks and recommends suppliers for the hood.

## A Christian View of Life and Death

How should we think about this provocative man, about doctor-assisted suicide, or about other forms of euthanasia? A believer in Jesus Christ has a very different view of death than Egbert or Kevorkian. Death in Scripture is clearly the judgment of God upon sin and has the idea of separation—separation from God and the separation of the body from the soul (physical death). God told Adam that if he ate of the tree in the garden he would die. When he and Eve ate, they both experienced the separation from God that resulted from sin, and they both eventually experienced physical death (see the narrative in Genesis 2 and 3). And, as Romans 5:12-21 makes clear, both sin and death have reigned over the human race ever since. But the death, burial, and resurrection of Jesus Christ dealt the death blow to sin and rendered death inoperative in the believer's life. Because Jesus conquered death through His resurrection, the believer need not fear death. Although the believer may die physically (the soul separated from the body), it is not permanent because of the promised resurrection. Hence, Paul can write in 1 Corinthians 15:54-55, "Death is swallowed up in victory. O death, where is your victory? O death, where is your sting?"

However, the believer in Jesus Christ faces death with tension. Paul gives us a window into this tension when he writes, "For to me, to live is Christ and to die is gain" (Philippians 1:21). Physical death means to be with Jesus and to have all the daily struggles, both physical and spiritual, ended. Although inexplicable, death is the door Christians go through to be with Christ. There is no other way, barring Christ's return for His church, for the believer to be with Christ. There is, therefore, the constant pull of heaven matched by the constant pull to remain and serve the Lord on earth. Death remains in the sovereign hand of God and when it comes, the believer, although anxious and perhaps frightened, trusts the words of Scripture: "To be absent from the body and to be at home with the Lord" (2 Corinthians 5:8).

At the same time, the Bible teaches that every person, believer and unbeliever, is inherently dignified and worthy of respect. Because men and women are created in the image and likeness of God (Genesis 1:26-27), it is always proper and ethically right to fight for life. Human life is sacred (Genesis 9:1-6) and no image bearer should be demeaned or cursed (James 3:9-10). To treat a human who bears God's image in an undignified manner, to wantonly destroy life, or to assume arbitrarily the position of authority over the life and death of another human, is to step outside of God's revelation. The Bible affirms the intrinsic worth and equal value of every human life regardless of its stage or condition. In a phrase, this is the Judeo-Christian view of life.

What are some implications of this high view of life? First, it seems logical that life is so valuable it should be terminated only when highly unusual considerations dictate an exception. In the Netherlands, for example, Parliament has empowered doctors to help individuals commit suicide if they are suffering from terminal illnesses and even if they are struggling with certain emotional/ mental disorders. In the United States, both Dr. Jack Kevorkian and Dr. Lawrence Egbert have each helped more than one hundred people commit suicide, some of whom were suffering from clinical depression. It is difficult to justify such actions from Scripture. Such practices cheapen life and treat the human as of little value and with no dignity. In short, to allow widespread euthanasia is to foster a culture of death.

Another implication of the Judeo-Christian view of life is that personhood is defined in biological terms. As defended in the previous chapter, a human is a person whose life begins at conception, not at birth. "Personhood" is not defined according to IQ, a sense of the future, a capacity to relate to other humans, or any other such criterion (more about these criteria later). The Bible consistently affirms that God creates life, defines its beginning at conception, and sustains that life. Humans who believe His Word will maintain the same view and always fight for life. To practice euthanasia in a pre-meditated manner (e.g., Kevorkian, Egbert, other forms of doctor-assisted suicide) violates the Bible's high view of life and can only be called homicide.

## The Quality of Life Ethic

Over the last several decades in Western civilization, especially in medicine but increasingly throughout the entire culture, a new ethic is replacing the Judeo-Christian ethic articulated above—i.e., the "quality of life" ethic. At its center, this new ethic places relative, rather than absolute, value on human beings. Let me cite several examples:

- Joseph Fletcher (cited in chapter two) argues that infanticide (killing of infants) and euthanasia are acceptable because human beings have a moral obligation to increase well-being wherever possible. "All rights are imperfect," he claims, "and can be set aside if human need requires it." Fletcher is a utilitarian who believes that objective moral norms are irrelevant in determining right and wrong. Only that which brings the greatest good to the greatest number is righteous. He goes on, "Human happiness and well-being are the highest good ... and ... therefore any ends or purposes which that ideal or standard validates are just right, good." Suicide and mercy killing are acceptable to Fletcher because "a morally good end can justify a relatively bad means."[1]

- For Joseph Fletcher, a human being, to meet the criteria of being truly human, must possess minimal intelligence, a sense of the future, of the past, a capacity to relate to others, and a balance between rationality and feelings. For example, a human with an IQ of 40 is questionably a person; one with an IQ of 20 or below is definitely not a person. Following Fletcher's logic, an infant, an adult or an elderly person with a degenerative brain disease would not meet these criteria and thus, forfeit the right to life.

• Michael Tooley, a philosopher, formerly at Stanford and now at the University of Colorado, thinks it unfortunate that most people use terms like "person" and "human being" interchangeably. Persons have rights but not every human being can properly be regarded as a person. His rule: An organism possesses a serious right to life only if it possesses the concept of a self as a continuing subject of experiences and other mental states and believes itself to be a continuing entity. For Tooley, infanticide is allowable up to a week after birth. Presumably, an elderly person with a degenerative brain disease would also not meet his criteria and thus, forfeit the right to life.[2]

• Peter Singer, Princeton University utilitarian philosopher, advocates something called Personism, an ethical philosophy of personhood. Singer believes that rights are conferred to the extent that a creature is a person, and Michael Tooley (see above) provides the relevant definition of a person. For example, Singer argues that fetuses and even newborn humans are not yet persons and do not, therefore, have the same rights as an adult human or any other person; most famously, he deprives them of the right to life. Singer also maintains that a member of the human species may not necessarily fit the definition of "person" and thereby not receive all the rights bestowed to a person, but animals might meet the definition and thereby the accompanying rights. Hence, Singer argues that "despite many individual exceptions, humanists have on the whole been unable to free themselves from one of the most central of these Christian dogmas: the prejudice of Speciesism."[3] Although a brilliant ethicist, Singer represents the natural results of surrendering the premise that humans have value because they bear God's image. He rejects that premise and ends up redefining personhood and even defends animals having the same rights as humans.

This new "quality of life" ethic is frightening. Rejecting any claim to ethical absolutes, this system flees to subjective criteria to define life's value and ends up justifying abortion, euthanasia, and infanticide. It violates all aspects of life's value as defined by the image of God concept and places humans in the seat of the sovereign God. Using subjective criteria, the quality of life ethic empowers other humans to decide who lives and who dies.

## Another Alternative: The Christian Hospice

This chapter has rejected the propensity of our culture to re-define "personhood" and justify euthanasia. However, what does a Christian do when a loved one is diagnosed with a terminal disease? What does one do if someone dear develops Alzheimer's disease or Huntington's disease? What if extremely painful cancer develops and the only promise is months or years of pain only to be followed by death?

There is no easy answer, but the Christian hospice movement is offering a powerful alternative for Christians today. Sometimes in a facility like a home or sometimes by providing care within the patient's own home, care for the dying patient is provided. It involves managing pain with drugs, giving loving comfort, and providing daily service to meet all human needs, whatever the specific situation. The care is complemented by the spiritual encouragement that comes from reading God's Word and other devotional material, prayer, and singing favorite hymns—all reminders of God's goodness and of the promise of eternal life. Death is not easy; as mentioned earlier in this chapter, the Christian approaches death differently than the unbeliever. The loving, empathetic, nail-scarred hands of Jesus are outstretched to welcome His child home to heaven. Hospice care provides the dignified alternative that honors God's creation—life—all the while preparing the dying saint for the promise that awaits him. It preserves the dignity of life that the "mercy killers" promise but cannot deliver.

## For Further Discussion

1. What does the term "euthanasia" mean? Define its various types.
   - Voluntary vs. Involuntary
   - Active vs. Passive
   - Direct vs. Indirect
   - Death with Dignity
   - Mercy Killing

2. Summarize the Judeo-Christian view of life and describe how this relates to the debate over euthanasia. Also, summarize how a Christian views death.

3. What is the "quality of life" ethic? How does it differ from the Judeo-Christian one? What particularly bothers you about this view?

4. How does the Christian hospice movement provide a biblical alternative to current practices of euthanasia? Research opportunities in your own community for hospice care.

## Notes

[1] Joseph Fletcher, *Situation Ethics* (Philadelphia: Westminster, 1966), 156-7.

[2] Michael Tooley, "A Defense of Abortion and Infanticide," *The Problem of Abortion*, Joel Feinberg, ed. (Nashville: Belmont, 1973), 51-91.

[3] Peter Singer, "Taking Humanism Beyond Speciesism," *Free Inquiry*, October/November 2004, 19-21.

# Bioethics: Reproductive and Genetic Technologies
# 6

The ethical issues associated with human reproductive and genetics technologies pose one of the greatest ethical challenges ever faced by genuine, biblical Christianity. These technologies have the potential to redefine the value and worth of human beings; indeed, they challenge the very uniqueness and sanctity of human life created in God's image. So serious are the complex and explosive ethical challenges of these technologies that government is crying for guidelines and advice on how to write legislation to deal with these issues. For example, in 1997, then-Governor Ben Nelson of Nebraska asked me to serve on the Human Genetics Technology Commission for the State of Nebraska. Chartered for one year, the commission's charge was to write a report offering guidelines and recommendations to assist his office and the legislature in making public policy to adequately address the thorny ethical challenges associated with human genetics technologies. In addition, both the federal government and private industry have funded The Human Genome Project, which mapped human DNA strands to identify every human gene and its function. The medical community now has an astonishing degree of knowledge about the human genome and, therefore, at least potentially, an unprecedented degree of control over humanity at virtually every stage of human development—from the embryo to old age.

Finally, the veritable revolution in human stem cell research has raised profound ethical questions never before faced by modern science. Is it acceptable to kill a human embryo to obtain the stem cells of that embryo? Is this ethically warranted? In short, what will we do with the human and genetic technologies now available and the resulting potential to control and manipulate other human beings? Will we be good stewards of this knowledge and control, or will unintended consequences result that no one ever envisioned? Does biblical Christianity have anything to offer when dealing with the ethical issues raised by these technologies?

To further illustrate the importance of thinking biblically about these technologies, consider the following case studies and ponder how you would respond:

- Suppose a Christian couple whom you know well came to you for some counsel. They are infertile and have shared with you the several options their doctor has proposed to solve their infertility problem. The doctor said the wife could be artificially inseminated using the husband's sperm or donor sperm from one of the myriad sperm banks throughout the United States. The doctor, likewise, shared with them a process known as *in vitro* fertilization (IVF), where several of the wife's eggs would be removed from her body and, through masturbation, the husband would provide the sperm needed to fertilize the eggs. (If the husband's sperm count is low, the doctor suggested, donor sperm could be used.) In a Petrie dish, the eggs would then be fertilized by the sperm, and the most robust embryos would be implanted in the wife's womb with the hope that one or more of the embryos would attach to her uterine wall and begin to grow. How would you respond? What counsel would you give?

- Suppose another couple, also struggling with infertility, sought your advice about hiring a surrogate to carry a baby, produced through artificial insemination using the husband's sperm (or a donor's sperm), which when born would, by contract, be turned over to the couple. How would you counsel them concerning this option? What ethical concerns are raised by surrogate motherhood?

- Suppose a Christian couple wants to have a child but is quite concerned that the child could have a genetic disorder. Using high-speed DNA sequencing, genome scientists can now deduce the DNA sequence of their fetus with 98 percent accuracy. Through this incredible procedure, parents can know the complete DNA of their child months before birth, enabling doctors to identify thousands of genetic diseases prenatally. Their doctor has also counseled them that if a genetic disorder (e.g., Down syndrome, Tay-Sachs disease or Marfan syndrome) is detected by this procedure, abortion is an option. Further, the doctor has also suggested that in not too many years they will actually be able to select the preferences they desire for their child (e.g., color of hair, height, athletic prowess, etc.). How would you counsel them? Should they go ahead with this sophisticated and very expensive procedure? Fundamentally, does such a procedure raise the ugly issue of eugenics?

- Suppose you have friends who are equally concerned about potential genetic disorders their children could have. They are concerned with the likely financial burden, as well as the probable hardship, of caring for a severely handicapped child. Their doctor has informed them of a procedure called preimplantation genetic diagnosis (PGD). Through *in vitro* fertilization, several of the wife's eggs are fertilized and allowed to divide for three days (at the eight-cell stage). The cells of the embryo are then tested for defective genes carried by the mother or the father. Embryos free of defective genes then are implanted in the mother's uterine wall or frozen. (Currently, PGD is used in about 10 percent of IVF procedures performed in the United States.) Should they use PGD? How would you counsel them? Could PGD be used to determine other traits or characteristics desired by parents? Could PGD become a tool for eugenics? Should the state set limits on what parents can do with the information gained from PGD?

Each one of these case studies illustrates a procedure or technique being used in the United States or the United Kingdom. All are quite expensive and some are not widespread in their use. But, they all represent the power of medical technology that is at the same time both awesome and frightening. As a result, the human race now possesses the power to control and manipulate life to a degree unimaginable only one generation ago. Guidance from God's Word is clearly needed.

## Modern Views of Humanity

Since the 18th-century Enlightenment, the Western view of humanity has undergone radical change, with the result that today humans are viewed as more like machines than image-bearers of God. The last two hundred years have weakened the biblical viewpoint that human beings, because they bear God's image, are unique and of infinite worth and value. As the biblical view has waned in the West, it has been replaced by a worldview that regards humanity as the product of the same impersonal forces that produced all life and focuses upon the quality of that life, not its infinite value. Because human beings are not unique, technology empowers humanity to improve, to control, and to manipulate. Seemingly, when it comes to technology, no ethical boundaries exist. Indeed, the mantra of the 21st-century seems to be: If it can be done technologically, it must be done. How did this develop? What is the origin of this tectonic shift in how humans are viewed? Several key historical figures have undermined the biblical worldview. For each of the following, humans are no longer the crown of God's creation; instead, humans are products of impersonal forces, not divine creation.

- Charles Darwin proposed the theory of evolution in his books *Origin of Species* (1859) and *The Descent of Man* (1872). According to the

Darwinian hypothesis, humans are merely products of the same force of natural selection that produced all other life forms; there is nothing unique about human beings. The impersonal forces of natural selection and random chance operating over vast amounts of time explain the origin of all life, including humans. If true, there are no ethical reasons for humans to be viewed as uniquely special or of infinite value.

- Sigmund Freud's theories postulated that all human behavior is unconsciously or subconsciously motivated. In many cases, these forces are remarkably powerful and deep in the subconscious. These forces explain human behavior and can only be discovered and dealt with through Freud's technique known as psychoanalysis. A devout atheist, Freud believed that religion was a sign of human weakness and evidenced a neurosis that needed curing. Ethically, Freud's system widened the boundaries for human behavior and beliefs, thereby enhancing the desire for greater human autonomy. Hence, Freud changed the entire discussion about sin and human accountability.

- Rejecting Freud's psychoanalysis, Benjamin Watson and B. F. Skinner (founders of modern behaviorism) argued that behavior is all you can really study in humans, and that human behavior is totally explained by heredity or the environment. Behaviorist techniques, they maintained, made it possible to control, manipulate, and alter human behavior. Freud's subconscious drives and forces were irrelevant and actually damaging, they argued. Furthermore, divine purpose or control played no role in the behaviorist's worldview.

- Today, sociologists and historians emphasize the social and historical forces that inform and explain virtually all human behavior, both individual and corporate. Each discipline seeks to discover universal laws that explain human behavior, with the goal of changing or manipulating the seemingly destructive human behavior they study. God, theology, or human sin plays little or no role in their respective disciplines or explanations for human behavior.

- Finally, geneticists and physiologists emphasize the genetic and chemical causes of human behavior and through medicine, pharmaceutical products, experimentation, or genetic surgery, seek to alter or change that behavior.

These various points of view minimize human accountability and seek to discover *the* explanation that covers all aspects of human behavior. An all-inclusive understanding of the forces that explain human behavior is the objective of each of those disciplines. A corollary is that once these forces are understood, it is necessary to control human behavior—to either improve it or to eliminate those aspects most harmful to the human race. Furthermore, in virtually all these viewpoints, God plays little or no role.

## Historical Developments Producing Openness Toward Human Manipulation

Again, since the 18th-century Enlightenment, several historical developments have produced a greater openness in Western civilization toward seeking to control and manipulate humans. First is a mechanistic view of human beings. For example, with organ transplants, the maintenance of organ donor banks, sperm donor banks, discussion about the harvesting of organs from cadavers, etc., it is not an immense step to view humans as near machines in which, when one part breaks down, another is ready to replace it. This is not medicine's intent, but the level of expectation is that somewhere a "part" exists for those who need it. What naturally follows is to view the human body as a machine, which, with proper maintenance and repairs, can keep on functioning. This logically results in a greater toleration of conception and genetic manipulation in the culture.

Another development is the technological control today over nearly every aspect of human life. We live in climate-controlled buildings, drive climate-controlled vehicles, access voluminous amounts of information via the Internet, can travel anywhere in the world in less than a day, and are living longer than at any time in recent human history. The reason? Technology. Because of human dependence on technology, there is the natural expectation that all human problems can ultimately be solved by technology, including infertility problems, health problems and emotional problems. Technology is the 21st century's savior!

Consequently, the concept of the scientific (or technological) imperative is the natural result. This concept assumes that because technology has made a seemingly beneficial procedure, invention, or practice possible, we as a civilization must go forward with it. The scientist's "can" becomes civilization's "ought." This is a powerful assumption now pervasive in Western thinking. For example, the invention of a deadly weapon or procedure, even something as unthinkable as chemical and biological warfare, relentlessly presses on until someone determines we must produce these weapons. That same logic drives conception and genetic technologies. Once a procedure is developed, it is nearly impossible to stop someone, somewhere, from using it. As a matter of stewardship before God, the scientific imperative needs to be challenged.

Another development producing this openness toward technological manipulation is the modern emphasis on pleasure and pain reduction as a virtual moral imperative. Think of common, everyday headaches. The typical drug store in the United States is filled with dozens of remedies that can treat headaches. Pain and discomfort are foreign to our lifestyle, and our expectation is that "there must be a pill somewhere for this ailment." This expectation transfers as well to the "good life" modern conveniences have produced. We expect—almost demand—ease, comfort, and daily pleasure in the forms of good food, entertainment, and self-indulgence. In the words of Francis Schaeffer, the values of "personal peace and affluence" drive Western civilization.[1] The result is an openness toward and a positive expectation from the technological manipulation of human beings.

The doctrine of the postmodern autonomous self is the final development within Western civilization that has fostered greater technological openness. "Autonomous" means "self-law." With the current view of law and with the persistent practice of defending human behavior in terms of rights and liberties (e.g., abortion, euthanasia, homosexuality), individualism has been elevated to an extreme level: Western civilization has embraced the proposition that the individual is nearly sovereign in his or her thinking and behavior. This view was epitomized in the Supreme Court's 1992 *Planned Parenthood v. Casey* case, which stated that "at the heart of liberty is the right of every individual to decide his or her own meaning of the universe...."[2] The sovereign self, therefore, determines the ethical value of reproductive and genetic technologies and does so as a matter of human liberty. In this postmodern culture, there are no universal ethical absolutes that trump the sovereign self.

## Types of Human Manipulation

In the case studies introducing this chapter, several examples of conception and genetic manipulation were cited. Dozens of other technological procedures are possible, but consider these three. Each one has significant ethical challenges that biblical Christianity cannot ignore:

**Cloning.** There are a variety of methods being used in animal research, but the core idea is to remove the DNA material of a cell's nucleus from one creature (e.g., a sheep) and place that material in the nucleus of a sheep embryo's cell nucleus, eventually producing a virtual duplicate of the original. For many years, cloning has been used to replicate DNA, cells, tissues, and plants. Technologically, this procedure could be done with humans but the social stigma against such a procedure remains strong. To do so with humans, especially to produce a human embryo through cloning, would violate the life, dignity, and rights of human beings. It is probable that this will gradually become acceptable but it is ethically dangerous. As the Nebraska Coalition for Ethical Research argues:

> When cloning is used to produce human embryos for medical research, a new human being is created solely to be destroyed for his or her cells. Cloning for the purpose of live birth produces a child who is wanted not for his or her own sake, but because he or she will carry traits that someone else values to duplicate. Producing human life by cloning reduces human beings to mere products and human procreation to a manufacturing process.[3]

Currently, researchers seek to make a distinction between "reproductive cloning" of human beings (cloning human embryos in order to produce live-born children) and "research/therapeutic cloning," which produces then destroys human embryos solely for research purposes. Both types of cloning may obscure the biological fact that these techniques produce a human embryo, which must be treated with dignity.

**Stem Cells**. Human embryonic stem cells are the master cells of the body. They have the capacity to produce more than two hundred different specialized cells that make up the adult human body. An embryo begins as a single cell zygote that starts to divide within hours of fertilization. After five days of development, the embryo is called a blastocyst. The cells of the early embryo (up to about the eight-cell stage) are totipotent, meaning that they can develop as a new and complete embryo. As these totipotent cells continue to divide, they differentiate and become more specialized cells called pluripotent stem cells, which can only produce the various specialized cells and organs of the body. To obtain the approximately one hundred pluripotent stem cells of the body at the blastocyst stage, researchers must, in effect, destroy the human embryo. This is ethically unacceptable because it is the destruction of a human life. For that reason, many researchers are calling for the use of adult stem cells (or umbilical cord or placental stem cells, which have the same qualities as adult stem cells). Human adult stem cells are a reasonable and ethically sound alternative. Human adult stem cells are multipotent, meaning they can differentiate into many different cell types, and some are showing pluripotent properties, meaning they theoretically differentiate into any of the two hundred cell types of the body. Current clinical uses and human trials of human stem cells include treatment for corneal scarring, stroke, heart attack, spinal cord injuries, breast cancer, diabetes, Parkinson's disease, arthritis, lymphoma, leukemia, melanoma, skin replacement, ovarian cancer, and many other forms of cancer and other diseases. As an important alternative to embryonic stem cells, adult stem cell research is ethical and should be supported because it does not violate the life, dignity, and rights of human beings.

**Frozen embryos.** Typically, when *in vitro* fertilization is used, excess embryos result and those not implanted into the mother's womb are frozen and stored in a growing number of clinics throughout the United States. Most estimates now suggest more than 500,000 frozen embryos exist in the United States alone. But the existence of these frozen embryos raises profound ethical and legal challenges. For example, in the spring of 1998, two couples—one divorced, one in the process—had been fighting over what to do with their fertilized ova—four- to eight-celled embryos—that were processed and frozen in happier times. In one case, the wife wanted the embryos implanted in her womb and, in the other case, the wife wanted the embryos destroyed. In both cases, the husbands fought in court to deny their wives' wishes. As this practice grows, the legal and ethical issues associated with frozen embryos become more complex. For example, the United Kingdom has a law that frozen embryos cannot be kept frozen for longer than five years. In 1997, more than three thousand frozen embryos were nearing that five-year threshold and faced destruction. The Vatican condemned the imminent destruction; couples and organizations from all over the world offered to "adopt" the embryos, but, in the end, they were destroyed. In Australia, a couple had previously frozen several embryos produced through *in vitro* fertilization but were tragically killed in a car accident. The legal authorities struggled to determine whether the embryos could legally inherit their parents' estate.

This book has argued that the human embryo is a person of value and worth. Therefore, the existence of frozen human embryos requires reflection and serious biblical thinking. Two conclusions seem warranted:

- Since one of our goals as Christians must be the protection of embryonic life, if "spare embryos" are produced through IVF and are not used for implantation, **it is ethically acceptable for these embryos to be frozen, provided that they are used, via future implantations, to produce a baby, not for experimentation.** (This, however, should not be understood to condone IVF, which I believe is ethically wrong. Once human embryos are produced through IVF, their existence is not an ethically neutral issue. Since God is concerned about the human embryo [see Psalm 139:16], as good stewards, we must be, too.)

- **Once the embryos are frozen, the major ethical guideline must be to protect them from harm.** It is ethically unacceptable to permit these frozen embryos to be used for experimentation of any kind. Rather, the only ethically sound option for frozen embryos is quick implantation in a mother's womb. Ethicists John and Paul Feinberg wrote, "...while we believe an IVF-conceived embryo has been produced by immoral means, once it exists, there is still an obligation to treat it morally. Killing it or allowing it to die is immoral. Freezing it and later implanting it...at the current state of our technology... seem the most likely ways to protect the child, and that must be the overriding concern."[4]

The case studies and scenarios presented in this chapter are just a sampling of the legal, medical, and ethical quagmires produced by reproductive and genetic technologies. Because of the crisis of moral authority in Western civilization, there is no absolute ethical framework to help address these issues. There is a desperate need for some guidelines rooted in God's revelation.

## Guiding Principles for Reproductive and Genetic Technologies

What follows is a list of guiding principles, sourced in Scripture, to deal with reproductive and genetic technologies and their results—both intended and unintended. Arguably not exhaustive, they offer some guidance, rooted in or inferred from God's Word. These guiding principles do not provide definitive answers to all the legal and ethical challenges raised in this chapter, nor do they suggest that all reproductive and genetic technologies should be discontinued or outlawed. Rather, they should be the starting point for discerning Christians as they think through and then seek to make wise decisions.

As argued in previous chapters, **human beings are created in God's image— the fundamental basis for human value and worth.** We can then stipulate that humans are always more valuable (intrinsically so) than all other created things. There is an essential, creation-order distinction between man and other created things (both living and non-living)—see Genesis 1 and 2. Hence, technology must always seek to preserve the worth, dignity, and value of all human beings, regardless of age or stage of development.

**Issues and practices associated with reproductive and genetic technologies fall under the stewardship responsibility of humanity to God.** In Genesis 1:26ff, God created humans—male and female—in His image and then gave them the responsibility to "be fruitful and multiply, and fill the earth, and subdue it; and rule over the fish of the sea and over the birds of the sky and over every living thing that moves on the earth" (v. 28). Verse 29 extends this dominion to plants, trees and seeds. God affirms this dominion status, although affected by human sin and rebellion, to Noah in Genesis 9:1-2. Because God is sovereign and humans have dominion status, human accountability is a necessary corollary. This matter of accountability has powerful implications when it comes to reproductive and genetic technologies. These technologies give humans power never realized before in history. But because of human depravity, it is difficult to be optimistic about the ultimate use of some of these technologies. In His common grace, God has permitted the human race to develop these technologies—but we must always remember that we are accountable to Him as to how we use them.

**The question of using these technologies is probably not so much whether to use them but how, when, and at what cost?** For example, *in vitro* fertilization involves multiple embryos produced in a Petrie dish. Several embryos are then implanted in the woman's womb. The remaining embryos are either destroyed or frozen. If life begins at conception (as the Bible stipulates), then destruction of the embryos is the destruction of life. Gender selection of children, which is now possible, could seriously upset the gender balance of any civilization. Empowering parents to exercise this kind of control seems unwise, even foolish. The challenges of human cloning are so immense that caution does not even seem wise; outright prohibition seems more so. In many of these technologies, we simply do not know the long-term effects of their widespread use. The sobering fact of human depravity looms over the use of these technologies.

As established in the previous chapter, **human life itself is of higher value than the quality of human life.** With the eternal perspective that Scripture gives, the quality of life ethic is faulty but seems to drive the current use of many of these technologies. Consider the examples of preimplantation genetic diagnosis and high-speed DNA sequencing mentioned in the case studies earlier. Both have the potential to create the "perfect child." Indeed, as a civilization, we seem bent on the pursuit of perfection. Ethicist Michael Sandel writes:

> In a world without givens, a world controlled by bioengineering, we would dictate our nature as well as our practices and norms. We would gain unprecedented power to redefine the good... The more successfully we engineered IQ and muscle-to-fat ratio, the more central these measures would become to our idea of perfection... But it w[ill] never be a perfect world. [5]

Because of sin, we live in an imperfect world, and until the new heaven and new earth, our fallen world will be characterized by disease, tragedies, accidents, and old age. The quality of life ethic, therefore, must never trump the infinite value of life ethic detailed in the Bible.

**From God's perspective, concern for the improvement of the "inner man" is always more important than concern for improvement of the "outer man."** No procedure or practice will prevent the inevitability of death. Perhaps that is why the Scripture gives focus to such issues as the fruit of the Spirit (Galatians 5:22-23) and the eight quality traits called the Beatitudes (Matthew 5:1-16). From God's perspective, these character traits are more paramount than using certain technologies to strive toward the goal of human perfectibility.

Carl Henry, years ago in his book, *Christian Personal Ethics* (1957), provided an important guideline for wise decision-making when it comes to reproductive and genetic technologies: "Whatever tends to overcome what would be a deterioration in the created order and seeks to restore what God purposed in Creation is on far safer grounds than all kinds of novel and experimental enterprise." [6] In other words, he argued that **there is clear biblical warrant for technologies that restore; there is no clear biblical warrant for manipulation toward perfection**—an insightful guideline in approaching some of the technologies discussed in this chapter.

When one views God's physical creation, one realizes that **values like unpredictability, variety, diversity, and uniqueness are central to God's creative work.** Some of the genetic technologies seem, at least potentially, to violate His values. Control over gender selection and other human features could produce a "sameness" that God did not intend. Does humanity know how to exercise wisely the kind of power and control that these procedures potentially bring? With the reality of sin ever before us, it is difficult to answer in the affirmative. Caution—methodical, meticulous caution—is needed in approaching the genetic minefield. That is why the prudent, biblical stance is that if a procedure will likely and eventually violate biblical guidelines, it is best to proceed on a very selective basis or not proceed at all.

Finally, human civilization must critically examine the scientific (technological) imperative. **Simply because society can pursue a particular medical, reproductive or genetic procedure does not mandate that it must!** Especially in the area of genetics, "can" does not mandate "ought." The potential for power and control and its obvious abuse mandates an examination of this imperative. Perhaps with some of these procedures, it would be wise to not do them at all.

This chapter has introduced bioethical issues fraught with both complexity and uncertainty. Rather than provide a comprehensive summary of all reproductive and genetic technologies, its goal has been to present an overview of the complexity and suggest some helpful guidelines inferred from God's Word.

## For Further Discussion

1. Review the role played by each in Western civilization in redefining man and his uniqueness in Western civilization:

- Darwin
- Freud
- Watson and Skinner

2. Summarize four or five developments in Western civilization that produced an openness toward reproductive and genetic manipulation.

3. Summarize some of the procedures discussed in the chapter. Following Carl Henry's dictum about restore rather than manipulate, which would you approve of and which not?

4. Discuss the scientific imperative. Is it valid? Explain.

5. List and summarize five of the guiding principles discussed at the end of the chapter.

## Notes

[1] Francis Schaeffer, *How Should We Then Live?* (Old Tappan, NJ: Revell, 1976), chapter 12.

[2] Russell Hittinger, "A Crisis of Legitimacy," *First Things*, November 1996, 26.

[3] Nebraska Coalition for Ethical Research, Omaha, NE. Position Papers on "Human Embryonic Stem Cell Research" and "Human Adult Stem Cell Research," both published in 2009.

[4] John Feinberg and Paul Feinberg, *Ethics for a Brave New World* (Wheaton, IL: Crossway, 1993), 240. (Also see Robert P. George and Christopher Tollefsen, *Embryo: A Defense of Human Life* [New York: Doubleday, 2008], 19-26.)

[5] Michael Sandel, *The Case Against Perfection: Ethics in the Age of Genetic Engineering* (Harvard: Belknap Press, 2007), 5.

[6] Quoted in Feinberg and Feinberg, 286.

# Human Sexuality

## 7

The doctrine of the autonomous self, mentioned in chapter six, with its panacea for personal rights and liberties, has resulted in a redefining of human sexuality in Western civilization. In so many categories of sexuality, what was once unthinkable gradually became debatable and is now acceptable. The ubiquity of pornography is enhanced by the Internet. Further, on TV sitcoms, in politics, business, entertainment and the arts, the homosexual lifestyle, for example, is common and basically a way of life.

In 2012, the President of the United States, Barack Obama, ended his administration's support of the Defense of Marriage Act, which defined marriage as between a man and a woman, and the President personally declared he supports same-sex marriage, seeing it as a human right. The natural consequence of this position, now widely accepted in the culture, is that you have the right to marry anyone you wish, regardless of gender. Marriage equality is today's civil rights campaign—just as was the black civil rights movement, the voting rights movement, and the women's rights movement earlier in U.S. history. Since it is now a right, when it comes to marriage, there is no possible basis for any state in this union to discriminate on the basis of sexual orientation. The speed with which American culture, law, and the government have accommodated to homosexuality and same-sex marriage has been stunning. Further, to even suggest that homosexuality and same-sex marriage are sin is to defend a view that the world sees as uneducated, rude, and stupid.

How should we think about this development? Is cultural accommodation to same-sex marriage of interest to God? How should genuine, biblical Christianity respond to this redefinition of the most basic institution of organized civilization? The goal of this chapter is to focus on what God has said about human sexuality and construct a strategy for impacting the culture on this matter.

## The Bible and Human Sexuality

It is a central axiom that marriage is fundamentally a public institution. Throughout all of human history, civilizations have always recognized the importance of marriage as a central organizing institution of the culture. Theologian Albert Mohler argues that "marriage regulates relationships, sexuality, human reproduction, lineage, kinship, and family structure. But marriage has also performed another crucial function—it has regulated morality."[1] As American culture is now redefining marriage to include same-sex unions, it also leads to a redefinition of reproduction and parenthood, while also producing a legal revolution and a completely new social order with a radically new morality. Indeed, Mohler strongly maintains that "marriage teaches morality by its very centrality to the culture. With a new concept of marriage comes a new morality, enforced by incredible social pressure, and, eventually, legal rights." Therefore, the church of Jesus Christ must focus in a fresh, new way on marriage as an institution created by God and on God's plan for human sexuality in all its fullness and beauty. The church must also develop pastoral approaches that are faithful to Scripture and then arm this generation of Christians to withstand the relentless cultural pressure and respond in ways that honor God.

One of those ways to do this is to articulate a biblical theology of sexuality. Stanton L. Jones, provost of Wheaton College, has written masterfully about this. Without a theology of sexuality, without a sexual ethic, we are, in the words of theologian David Bentley Hart, "... first and foremost, heroic and insatiable consumers, and we must not allow the specters of transcendent law or personal guilt render us indecisive. For us, it is choice itself, and not what we choose, that is the first good."[2] This obsession with autonomy ("self-law") consumes the 21st-century person who has no transcendent standards. Consequently, sexuality becomes the foundation of personal identity and pursuit of selfish, self-centered pleasure its passion. But there is a positive, truthful vision of sexuality—and it is found in the Bible. Permit me, then, to summarize Jones's theology of sex:

- **We are embodied.** To be human is to be a physical, biological creature. Christians view all of physical existence, from the grandeur of the cosmos to the particularity of the human body, as the good creation of a benevolent God. Physical existence is not divine, but it is good. We are more than bodies, but we are bodies—and we will live forever as a soul-body unit in our glorified, resurrected bodies.

- **We are sexual beings.** We are gendered, and we are sexual beings. Genesis 1 and 2 declare God's creation of gendered people to be the divine purpose, with both sexes made in the image of God and humanity corporately, male and female, declared to be very good. Scripture extols the physical pleasures of sexual union (Proverbs 5) and links eroticism explicitly with romantic love and intimacy (Song of Solomon). The Apostle Paul sternly admonishes married couples to fulfill one another's sexual needs and does so in a re-markably egalitarian fashion (1 Corinthians 7:1-6). Jones writes: "Our sexuality is expressed in but not reduced to the sexual experiences of marriage. All persons are fully sexual as gendered beings with uniquely male or female bodies, beings with sensations, desires, and gender-grounded emotional and cognitive capacities. Gender is only one facet of sexuality, and gender itself is a construct with many biological, psychological, emotional and relational dimensions." [3]

- **We are relational.** Genesis teaches us to think of human nature as fundamentally relational. Even though Adam lived in a perfect environment, God declared it not good for him to be alone. So God created a perfect partner, a complement in every way to him. Romantic love, as with Adam and Eve (Genesis 2:24-25), became an important way that the relational reality of being human was experienced. That is still true today.

- **We are made in God's image.** The way Genesis 5 mirrors the language of Genesis 1:26ff is stunning. The conception and birth of a son to our primal parents parallels the way God "fathered" the first humans. God's image cannot be reduced to simple procreation, but the act of human procreation is somehow part of what it means to be in the image and likeness of God.

- **We are broken and twisted.** Our sexual longings are grounded in our good capacities for union, love and pleasure, but they are always tainted with selfishness, sensuality, and the desire to dominate. "This is why we experience a deep sense of conflict in our sexuality. We know the beauty, potential and realized good of our sexual natures, but we never experience that good distilled and pure." [4]

- **We encounter objective reality when we have sex.** Sexual intercourse creates a one-sex union. The Creation Ordinance, Christ's teaching on divorce, and such pivotal passages as 1 Corinthians 6 and 7 teach us that God made sexual intercourse to create and sustain a permanent, one-flesh union in a male-female married couple. "The fact that intercourse creates a one-flesh union profoundly challenges our individualism.... We learn from Paul that the marriage union testifies to something bigger than itself (Ephesians 5:32). All Christians participate in a mystical body, which is truly the body of Christ (1 Corinthians 12) and the consummation of history is not the redemption of a gaggle of individuals but a marriage between the Bridegroom Lamb and his (collective singular) Bride....There is more to sex than meets the eye."[5]

- **We are souls under construction.** The Christian vision of personhood means that the true self is both discovered and formed. Proper self-formation occurs when our self is submitted to God, who transforms us as we obey His revealed will and we abide in relationship with a Savior who indwells and molds us. A self that is only discovered is an undeveloped, impoverished self. "A self that is discovered and then formed in the joyful, painful, humbling and intimate process of celebrating the gift of sexuality God has given, dying to one's sin nature, and living in costly obedience to God will be the truest and most real self."[6] Christian ethicist Gilbert Meilander has argued that "to be human...is to learn of our embodied, mortal life, the limits of those whose being opens to God. It is to acknowledge, honor, and esteem the particular place—between beasts and God—that we occupy in the creation."[7]

- **God's Creation Ordinance.** When discussing homosexuality and same-sex marriage, evangelical Christians usually point to the Levitical code, to Sodom and Gomorrah, or to Paul's statements in the New Testament. I believe this is an error. The proper place to begin thinking about both issues is Genesis 2, God's Creation Ordinance. After giving clear instructions to Adam about his stewardship of the garden, God concluded that it was not good for Adam to be alone (v. 18). To prove this to Adam, God brought all the animals before him to name (vv. 18-20). Although this established his authority over the animals, it also served as an object lesson for Adam: He was the only creature of God truly alone. So, God created the woman as his complement, his helper (vv. 21-23).

Moses then offered a theological commentary on what God did with Adam and Eve (vv. 24-25). First, God established the paradigm for marriage. The man is to "leave" his family with the conscious understanding that he is establishing a new family unit. Second, that means "cleaving" (like glue) to his wife. Third, by separating from his family and because of the unqualified commitment to his wife, he and his wife will, for the rest of their lives, be in the process of "becoming one flesh." The one-flesh concept does symbolize the sexual intercourse that physically unites them as husband and wife, but it also symbolizes the merging of two personalities, male and female, into a complementary whole. Their personalities, their idiosyncrasies and their uniqueness all remain; they do not cease. Instead, these two totally different human beings merge into a perfect complement where both—now united together in marriage—serve God in their integrity.[8]

In verse 25, Moses further commented that Adam and Eve were "naked" and not "ashamed." They were so totally "other-centered" that they did not think of self, only of one another. We can properly infer that their sexual oneness was characterized by no shame or discomfort either. Their physical love was beautiful and fulfilling; no selfish or carnal lust was present. The wonder of romantic love was perfectly modeled by this first marriage.

What do we learn from the Creation Ordinance? How does this passage establish the model for a proper understanding of both human sexuality and marriage? Allow me to suggest two conclusions:

- When Jesus and Paul deal with questions of marriage or human sexuality, they always refer back to this Creation Ordinance of Genesis 2:18-25. See Matthew 19:1-12, Mark 10:1-12, and 1 Corinthians 7:10-11. What is stated in these verses transcends, culture and time. They constitute God's ideal for sexuality and marriage.

- Marriage is to be monogamous and heterosexual. From this passage it is impossible to justify polygamy or homosexuality. It is the standard, the ideal, for all marriages. Therefore, one simply cannot justify "same-sex" marriages. This is not an option for humans.

With this standard established for marriage in the Creation Ordinance, the other scriptural passages dealing with human sexuality are all measured against Genesis 2. Each details that fornication, adultery, bestiality or homosexuality are all an aberration, a radical departure from God's clear standard.

- Genesis 19:1-11—This is the story of Sodom, which God utterly destroyed with fire. Homosexual commentators see the sin of the men in this passage as a violation of Ancient Near Eastern hospitality codes. But verse 5 and Lot's response in verse 8 demonstrate unequivocally that homosexual relations are what was on the minds of these men. It is a deliberate departure from God's clear revelation in Genesis 2.

- Leviticus 18:22, 29 and 20:13—Homosexual commentators often argue that we do not keep most other parts of the Levitical law, so why emphasize this one so adamantly. Although Jesus' finished work on Calvary's cross did render inoperative much of the Levitical law and practices (the argument of the Book of Hebrews), issues of human sexuality transcend the law because of the Creation Ordinance of God in Genesis 2. What God says in Leviticus 18 and 20 is tied clearly to His standard established at creation. Homosexuality is ethically wrong.

- Romans 1:26-27—In this passage, Paul's argument about the debased sexual practices cited in the verses hangs on his use of the word "natural." Homosexual commentators argue that Paul is condemning unfaithfulness in the homosexual relationship, not homosexuality itself. However, "natural" and "unnatural" can only be understood as departure from or adherence to some standard that determines what natural and unnatural is. That standard can only be the standard established in God's Creation Ordinance in Genesis 2.

- 1 Corinthians 6:9-10—To motivate the Corinthians out of their spiritual lethargy and complacency, in this passage Paul lists the various categories of sinners God will keep out of His kingdom. His goal is that they examine themselves. Among those listed are "effeminate" and "homosexuals." Paul Feinberg argues that these two Greek words focus on both the active and the passive partner in the homosexual relationship. The emphasis of the passage is not on unfaithfulness to the homosexual partner, as the homosexual commentators contend, but on the very homosexual act itself.[9]

- 1 Timothy 1:10—Here Paul also condemns homosexuality as contrary to "sound teaching." The issue is not unfaithfulness to a homosexual partner but engaging in something that violates God's clearly revealed standard. In this case, what is "sound teaching" is God's revelation in His Creation Ordinance, just as "liars," "kidnappers," "perjurers" and others violate His standards revealed elsewhere (the Ten Commandments, for example).

In summary, as with all sexual activity outside of marriage, the Bible resoundingly condemns the homosexual lifestyle as contrary to the ethical standard God establishes in His Creation Ordinance. Without some benchmark to settle the ethical debate on human sexuality, heated confrontations within the culture will continue. God's Word provides that benchmark; obedience is the only acceptable response.

## Causation: Genetic or Environmental?

Among psychologists and scholars today, much of the debate over the causation of homosexuality appears settled. Is it genetically determined or is it environmental? Those in the gay community argue passionately that being gay is genetically determined. Those in the religious gay community say that it is God's gift. To try to change your giftedness sexually would be an affront to God. Simon LaVay, himself a homosexual, has done tests on cadavers who were homosexual and has found that the pituitary gland of these homosexual men is larger than non-homosexual men. Jeffrey Satinover, in his book, *Homosexuality and the Politics of Truth,* presents compelling evidence that questions LaVay's research and the research and data of all claims that homosexuality is a genetically caused.[10] Indeed, Satinover's conclusions seem to show rather conclusively that homosexuality is a learned way of life (a choice) produced by circumstances in life. This is not a very popular position today, especially in many universities and even among those of the American Psychiatric Association (APA), which no longer views homosexuality as pathology in need of treatment.

Satinover's book is a powerful indictment of the politically correct agenda driving so many professional organizations, as well as the national gay movement itself. Other serious researchers, some of whom are evangelical Christians, still argue for some kind of genetic role in the causation of homosexuality.[11] Hence, early 21st-century science is not definitive in answering the question of causation. Yet, in one sense causation is irrelevant to God's view of any deviation from God's Creation Ordinance. The Bible still condemns it and God's power is still sufficient to overcome it.

## A Word about Pornography

The seventh largest industry in America is pornography. According to a recent *60 Minutes* broadcast (spring of 2005), Americans now spend more than $10 billion a year on "adult entertainment" products. In addition, the Internet has spawned the largest number of pornographic options in human history. Theologian Albert Mohler suggests that "Internet pornography is the crack cocaine of the sex trade. Men and boys, enticed by pornographic images and stimulation, are drawn deeper and deeper into patterns of lust and sexual seduction. Women, young and old, are increasingly drawn into Internet chat rooms, where simulated sensuality is combined with simulated intimacy."[12] Ron Luce, in his book, *Battle Cry for a Generation: The Fight to Save America's Youth,* argues that "90% of 8- to 16-year olds have viewed porn online."[13] The result is that teens can no longer distinguish between entertainment and debauchery, wholesome sex within marriage and perversion. Indeed, perversion is so mainstream that teens (and adults) often take in a daily diet of filth through TV, movies, and even advertisements.

The effects of pornographic addiction are clear: (1) Like all sin, it entices and deceives, never delivering what it promises—fulfillment and joy. (2) It can destroy other-centered, *agape* love within marriage. Teens who are addicted to pornography before marriage will often feel its effects after they marry. (3) It degrades and dehumanizes as it becomes addictive. (4) It can lead to perversion and promiscuity. (5) It fosters sexual isolation, not intimacy within marriage. (6) It can lead to rape. (7) It can produce violence and abuse. The church, therefore, must face this brutal reality and offer solutions. Building on the theology of sexuality discussed above, church leaders must also affirm that the Bible also condemns lust (e.g., Matthew 5:28; Ephesians 2:3; 1 Thessalonians 4:3-8; 2 Timothy 2:22; Titus 3:3) and declares that outside of marriage, sexual abstinence is the only option for the Christian (e.g., Exodus 20:14; 22:16-17; Proverbs 23:27; 1 Corinthians 5:1; 6:9, 13, 18).

The church must also address masturbation, because almost always it accompanies pornographic activity. Scripture never directly addresses this issue, but it is possible to infer some clear biblical principles. Certainly, where masturbation involves lust or a desire for someone other than one's spouse, Scripture speaks clearly—it is wrong. If masturbation prevents a spouse from fulfilling one's duties within marriage, it is wrong (see 1 Corinthians 7:1-7). In short, self-stimulation is ethically suspect and plays no role in a healthy sexual relationship within marriage. As with all other aspects of sexuality outside of marriage, abstinence is the only option.

Since there is pornographic addiction within the church, what should effective leaders do? They must affirm and model that God places sexual pleasure within the holy covenant of marriage, combining restraint with passion, pleasure with protection, and sense with sensibility. The church must combat the culture's lie that being a man is all about sexual conquest. Manhood, the culture says, is associated with the capacity to use girls and women for personal pleasure. What a perverted lie! For those who have fallen into the morass of pornography, there must be repentance and an absolute, daily dependence on God. Facing this reality is the necessary first step. Second, those who struggle with pornographic addiction must develop a personal strategy for holiness (see Ephesians 4:22-32). Daily, there must be the decisive act of putting away the old addictions and passions, the renewing of the mind through saturation with Scripture, and the decisive act of putting on the "new," with its righteousness and holiness. Hence, for example, there must be a resolute change in the use of the Internet, in magazines read, and in TV programs watched. One cannot be passive in the pursuit of holiness! Third, there must be accountability. For someone addicted to pornography, a friend, a pastor or a relative must have the freedom to ask hard questions and insist on accountability. There are no "lone rangers" in dealing with sin. There must be the fellowship and the encouragement that comes from being around other believers who can promote "love and good deeds" (Hebrews 10:24).

The church, and especially effective youth ministry, cannot ignore the scourge of pornography. Pornographic addiction is real and it is infiltrating the church. Ron Hutchcraft has an excellent resource to aid youth ministries—the DVD, "Sex at its Best! A Positive Morality for Today's Youth." Also, his book, *The Battle for a Generation*, provides excellent tools to combat this deceptive blight. Computer programs such as "SafeEyes" and "EtherShield" provide effective tools to block pornographic sites on home and networked computers.

## Homosexuality and the Church: Confronting and Discipling the Homosexual

In 1985, Don Baker published a book, *Beyond Rejection*, which chronicles the story of Jerry, who struggled with homosexuality from his childhood through seminary and into marriage. It remains a valuable tool for ministering to the gay or lesbian, for it provides a much-needed window into the extreme difficulties of this struggle and yet the hope provided by Jesus Christ. It is must reading for the church, for it provides the balance of truth and compassion. Based on the balance brought by this book, let me suggest several action points for ministering to the gay and lesbian within our culture:

- Remember that to the gay and lesbian subculture, evangelicals are the enemy! Because the Bible speaks so clearly on this issue and evangelicals reflect that truth, there is no room for compromise or discussion. Patience, love, and compassion are needed as relationships are developed.

- Remember that homosexuality is a sin. That is the point of the earlier part of this chapter. But it is not the "worst" sin. God's grace is completely sufficient to deal with this bondage but, although scandalous, it is not singularly worse than others.

- Unconditional love is an absolute requirement in ministry to those in bondage to this sin. Compassion, empathy, patience, and commitment for the long haul are necessary prerequisites. The reality is that many will fall back into the lifestyle, even after conversion to Jesus Christ. That is why organizations like Exodus International are so critical. A ready-made support group of encouragers and accountability are central to this organization's ministry.

- Repentance must always be the goal. There must be the complete break with the past and with the lifestyle. There is no compromise or middle ground available. Here again, Exodus International and other such ministries are so central to ministering to the homosexual.

Human sexuality is being redefined within Western civilization. Somehow the church of Jesus Christ must be able with one hand to declare that aberrant sexual lifestyles are morally and ethically wrong, while with the other reaching out the hand of love, acceptance, and compassion. Only Jesus Christ, working through His Spirit, can enable and empower His church to accomplish this most difficult and seemingly impossible task.

## For Further Discussion

1. What does the author mean by the Creation Ordinance when it comes to human sexuality? How do the following passages relate to it?

   - Genesis 19:1-11

   - Leviticus 18:22, 29; 20:13

   - Romans 1:26-27

   - 1 Corinthians 6:9-11

   - 1 Timothy 1:11

2. Summarize the debate between genetic vs. environmental causes of homosexuality. Which do you find most compelling?

3. Summarize how this ethical issue is impacting the church. Do some investigation about your own church's position on this issue, especially if you come from a mainline denominational church.

4. What attitude should Christians have toward homosexuals? Suppose one of your children believes he or she is a homosexual. How would you respond? How should this issue be handled in the church?

5. How would you counsel someone addicted to pornography?

6. Does this issue have anything to say about the importance of children having both male and female role models from an early age? Comment on any personal experience you may have had with children.

# Notes

[1] Albert Mohler, Jr., "The Challenge of Same-Sex Unions," *Tabletalk*, April 2012, 82.

[2] Quoted in Stanton L. Jones, "How to Teach Sex," *Christianity Today*, January 2011, 36.

[3] Jones, 37.

[4] Jones, 38.

[5] Ibid.

[6] Jones, 39.

[7] Gilbert Meilander, *Neither Beast nor God: The Dignity of the Human Person* (New York: New Atlantis Books, 2009), 10.

[8] See Alan Ross, Jr., *Creation and Blessing* (Grand Rapids, MI: Baker, 1988), 117-129, and John Piper and Wayne Grudem, *Recovering Biblical Manhood and Womanhood* (Wheaton, IL: Crossway, 1991), 95-112.

[9] John Feinberg and Paul Feinberg, *Ethics for a Brave New World* (Wheaton, IL: Crossway, 1993), 199-201.

[10] Jeffrey Satinover, *Homosexuality and the Politics of Truth* (Grand Rapids, MI: Baker, 1996), 78-81.

[11] See this helpful article: Herbert Wray, "The Politics of Biology," *US News and World Report*, April 21, 1997, 72-80.

[12] Albert Mohler, Jr., "The Pornographic Seduction," *Tabletalk*, June 2005, 62-63.

[13] Ron Luce, *Battle Cry for a Generation: The Fight to Save America's Youth* (Colorado Springs: Cook Communications Ministries, 2005), 12.

# The Christian and Politics
## 8

Should Christians vote? Should they run for political office? Is it proper for Christians to engage in civil disobedience? What exactly is the ethical obligation the believer owes to the state? Does the Bible speak to any of these questions? This chapter will argue that Scripture gives clear guidelines for all of these questions, giving the Christian a framework for making an impact in the political arena for righteousness and the kingdom of God.

### Christian Obligation Toward the State

It is the New Testament's clear teaching that the Christian does have an obligation toward the state. This is the central point of Jesus' teaching in Mark 12:13-17, where, when questioned about paying taxes to Rome, He answers that we "render to Caesar the things that are Caesar's, and to God the things that are God's." We owe obligation obviously to God and His kingdom but also to the state because He created it and it serves His purpose.[1] This passage makes clear the obligation to the state stems from being a member of the state.

The Apostle Paul expands on Jesus' argument in Romans 13:1-7 when he argues that the Christian is to submit to government because God established it. No ruler, president, prime minister, or tyrant has power that did not first come from God (Daniel. 4:17-25). In verses 3 and 4 of Romans 13, Paul also argues that the state is to administer justice and thwart evil. This is the principal reason that God created government in the first place (Genesis 9:5-7). Paul seems to imply that this function of the state is actually conducive to the spread of the Gospel.

The final reason for the Christian's obligation toward government is found in 1 Timothy 2:1-7. Here the believer is instructed to pray for those in authority in the state, in order that "we may lead a tranquil and quiet life in all godliness and dignity" (v. 2). As C. E. B. Cranfield argues from verses 3-7, "It is implied that God wills the state as a means to promoting peace and quiet among men, and that God desires such peace and quiet because they are in some way conducive to men's salvation."[2]

### The Christian's Responsibility to the State

That Christians have a responsibility toward the state is now clear, but what exactly is the content of that obligation?[3] First, the believer owes the state respect. Romans 13:7 and 1 Peter 2:17 both admonish the Christian to honor and respect government as ministers of God who have been ordained by Him and are accountable to Him for their solemn trust of promoting justice and thwarting evil. Respect involves treating with full seriousness even individuals who have no respect for the office or their high calling to that office. That dimension, therefore, necessitates administering rebuke and calling to account those rulers who abuse their high office or treat with contempt the office itself. In the United States, respect would mean utilizing the constitutional means of impeachment to judge any federal official who has committed treason, bribery, or other "high crimes or misdemeanors."[4]

Second, the believer owes the state, its agents, and its duly enacted laws obedience (Titus 3:1; 1 Peter 2:13-17; Romans 13:1-7). Jesus paid the temple tax and Paul apologized for speaking disrespectfully to a ruler. Further, Jesus' birth occurred in Bethlehem because Joseph was obedient to an oppressive government demanding a tax-assessing edict. Yet the New Testament mandate is neither slavish nor absolute; we see Peter and John defying the Sanhedrin's order to stop preaching. The issue apparently to them was clear: We obey the state until it is a sin to obey the state. Here civil disobedience was not merely permitted by God's Spirit; it was demanded (Acts 4:19ff; 5:29). If the government therefore commands something that God forbids or forbids something that God commands, we must disobey. That disobedience cannot involve violence nor vandalism, actions that contradict prudence and civil order.

Thus, disobedience should never be taken lightly or with undue haste. Christians do have a higher law than that of human government. But God gives human governments in the main His seal of approval and disobedience to them should be considered with great caution. Lynn Buzzard offers seven questions the believer should ask when facing the possibility of disobedience to the state:

- How directly and immediately does the opposed government policy contradict an unequivocal biblical teaching?

- What is the counsel of the Christian community about this policy? Where do godly leaders rank it among threats to the faith that must be addressed? What do they say about what the faithful person's response ought to be? To what extent have legal, alternative protests been exhausted?

- What harms to society and order are likely to result from the considered act of civil disobedience, and how do these harms compare with the desired benefits?

- Will the form of civil disobedience be one which will evidence moral consistency and further proper respect for principled law and a moral society?

- To what extent will the "witness" be heard and understood by the public and by government authorities?

- To what extent are the acts central to maintaining my integrity as a person? To what extent may they reflect personal frustration and anger rather than a principled response?

- To what extent does the idea for the act of civil disobedience issue from thought sources alien to a biblical worldview? Is it based upon biblical principles about the uses of power and coercion, the witness of the cross, and the sovereignty of God, or is it based upon purely naturalistic, humanistic principles?[5]

Third, the believer must pay taxes (Mark 12:13-17; Matthew 22:15-22; Luke 20:20-26; Romans 13:6-7). Jesus makes the payment of taxes the fundamental mark of obligation to the state, regardless of its morality or ethical bankruptcy. This is clear because Jesus and Paul were both writing of tax payment to the Roman empire, a corrupt, evil, and ethically repulsive state.

Fourth, the believer must pray for those in authority (1 Timothy 2:1ff). Such praying for civil authorities is an essential part of the debt owed, whether the official is pagan or Christian, religiously indifferent or anti-religious, just or unjust. I am often frustrated by Christians who relentlessly criticize governmental officials but rarely, if ever, pray for those officials. God can use praying to effect righteousness in the state's laws or in bringing an unbelieving governmental official to Jesus Christ. Constructive criticism and calling the state to accountability need to be balanced with fervent, persevering prayer.

## Inferences for a Christian Living in a Democracy

These, then, are the four ethical obligations the Christian owes to the state but out of these obligations grow certain other inferences that are especially acute for the Christian who lives in a democracy. First, the Christian should vote. In normal circumstances, according to Cranfield, failure to vote "is to abandon one's share of responsibility for the maintenance of the state as a just state and therefore a dereliction of one's duty as a Christian." Second, the Christian should keep oneself as fully and reliably informed as possible concerning political, social, and economic issues. This necessitates diligent reading of newspapers, news magazines, careful watching of television news broadcasts, and reasoned, balanced discussion of such issues with friends and colleagues.

Third is criticism of the government, its policies, and its agents in light of God's revelation. The Bible becomes the grid through which the Christian evaluates the state's actions and policies; the believer is willing to call the state to righteousness in light of God's Word. Finally, the Christian should work for just and righteous laws and oppose those policies and decisions that are unjust and unrighteous. In a democracy, this involves activities such as working for candidates who support justice and righteousness and supporting, through calling and writing letters, legislation that reflects genuine, biblical righteousness.

## Christian Involvement in Government and Politics

Increasing involvement in politics and government has grave dangers for the Christian. To provide the maximum impact for righteousness in government, a proper and balanced perspective is needed. This necessitates ridding ourselves of what Chuck Colson calls a "starry-eyed view of political power." [7] Some Christians think that by marshaling a Christian voting bloc Christ's kingdom on earth can be established. The external and limited good that political power can achieve should not be confused with the internal and infinite good that God's grace produces. Further, there is danger in what Colson calls the "political illusion," the notion that all human problems can be solved by political institutions. This is idolatrous to believe because the Bible declares the root problem of society is spiritual. What the Christian seeks through government is justice, not power. Our goal is, therefore, to move the culture toward the righteousness of God's revelation. The job of total spiritual transformation is the role of Christ; through the church, not the state.

How then does the Christian decide what to support and what to reject in politics? How does one decide whom to support in elections? For what kinds of laws should the believer work and fight? Robert Dugan, former director of the National Association of Evangelicals, suggests five major principles to guide the Christian in assessing potential candidates and laws:

- **The pre-eminence of religious liberty**—Any candidate or legislation that restricts the practice of religious faith should be resisted.

- **The protection of life as sacred**—Candidates or legislation that treat life frivolously or that seek to destroy it (e.g., abortion, euthanasia, infanticide) should be resisted and defeated.

- **Provision of justice for all**—Candidates and legislation must reflect God's concern for justice and equity. Reading the Book of Amos is convincing evidence that God desires government to promote laws that protect the poor and disadvantaged from exploitation and oppression.

- **Preservation of the traditional family**—One of the clear teachings of the Bible is that the family is a critical institution to God. Legislation that negatively impacts the family should be rejected. For example, tax legislation that promotes single-parent families or penalizes a father for living with his family is counterproductive. The promotion of same-sex marriages runs counter to God's revelation and should be rejected.

- **The promotion of Judeo-Christian values in education and legislation**—For example, values of honesty, integrity, personal responsibility, and accountability can be easily undermined by a leader who wantonly lies and shows disrespect for the law. Fraud, bribery, and corruption undermine public trust and confidence and are terribly destructive. Education must reinforce the values of parents and not undermine their authority (Deuteronomy 6:1-10).[8]

Christians, then, as salt and light (Matthew 5:13-16), should seek to effect righteous change in the culture through the political process, not because the kingdom comes from Washington, but because God expects us to be serving and waiting (1 Thessalonians 1:9-10).

## The Role of the Church

Should the church as a local body of believers function as a political caucus, a political coalition, or any other level of political activity? Some Christians believe local churches should not be involved in political activities. They reason, first, that the laws of the United States are clear concerning local churches not engaging in direct political activities (endorsing a particular candidate). To do so would violate (and possibly result in loss of) the non-profit status for the organizations. Second, the Bible gives no mandate, or even logical inference, for local church political activity. Third, there is no evidence of the early church being involved in politics. Furthermore, the local church often lacks the necessary expertise for reasoned political involvement and can even find its witness severely harmed. The local church is a spiritual body, rooted in God's revelation. Christians, individually, should be involved in the political arena but the local church will do so to its peril.

On the other hand, some Christians believe the local church is not ordained as a political body, yet because individuals are charged with this responsibility the collective group involvement can most certainly impact politics and government. Therefore, local churches should be involved with political issues relating to morality and justice.

Christians walk a careful balance between understanding the Christian obligation toward the state and seeking to influence that state for righteousness and justice. The two spheres of the Christian's life—the church and the state—must be kept in balance. Each has a divine job to do; neither should encroach upon the responsibility of the other.

## For Further Discussion

1. Discuss why Mark 12:13-17 is foundational for the Christian's obligation toward the state.

2. What are three reasons the author suggests for the Christian's obligation to the state?

3. Summarize the specific political responsibility of each of these (when possible use Scripture references):

   • Respect

   • Obedience

   • Payment of taxes

   • Prayer

4. Should a Christian ever actively disobey the state? Is there room for civil disobedience? Is there biblical evidence for this? What does Lynn Buzzard suggest as guidelines for this difficult topic?

5. What are some inferences the author suggests for Christian living in a democracy?

6. What is the "political illusion"? What are some guidelines that Robert Dugan suggests for Christian involvement in politics?

7. Should the church as a local body ever support a political candidate? Should it form a political caucus? Summarize the author's points.

## Notes

[1] Charles Colson, *Kingdoms in Conflict* (Grand Rapids, MI: Zondervan, 1987), 109-121.

[2] C. E. B. Cranfield, "The Christian's Political Responsibility According to the New Testament," *Scottish Journal of Theology* 15 (1962): 179.

[3] Ibid., 176-192.

[4] See United States Constitution, Article 2, Section 4.

[5] Lynn Buzzard, "Civil Disobedience," *Eternity*, January 1987, 19-25.

[6] Cranfield, 185.

[7] Charles Colson, "The Political Illusion," *Moody Monthly*, October 1994, 22-25.

[8] Quoted in Bob Reynold, "Onward Christian Voters," *Moody Monthly*, September/October 1996, 23-25.

# The Ethical Challenges of War and Capital Punishment
# 9

War and capital punishment are perhaps the most excruciating ethical challenges for the Christian. As chapters four and five have shown, life is of infinite value to God and must always be respected and valued. Yet, many Christians argue that it is proper and just to engage in war and kill other human beings created in God's image. Furthermore, Christians are involved in making and then deploying weapons of mass destruction. Is this justifiable in terms of God's Word? Finally, many Christians argue strongly for the right of the state to take the life of another human being who commits premeditated murder and other especially heinous crimes. How do we biblically approach these difficult questions?

## A Matter of Definition

The difference between kill and murder is quite critical in a discussion about war. Many Christians do not see a difference between these two terms but the Bible does. The King James Version renders Exodus 20:13 as "Thou shalt not kill," while the New International Version renders the same verse, "You shall not murder." The Hebrew term in this case, *rasah*, does mean to kill, but it is never used in relation to animals and is always associated with murder. Furthermore, it is never used of killing an enemy in battle.[1] Therefore, not all life-taking is murder.

Two examples exist in the Old Testament. First is Genesis 9:6— "Whoever sheds man's blood, by man his blood shall be shed, for in the image of God He made man." God gave this to Noah before the Mosaic Law and was restated in Numbers 35 as part of the Mosaic Code. As Charles Ryrie states, "One can conclude that when the theocracy [of Israel] took the life of a murderer (i.e., one who violated the sixth commandment) the state (and particularly those who actually performed the execution) was not guilty of murder."[2] The second example is the conquest of Canaan. In Deuteronomy 20:10-18, God revealed His rules for war. It is clear from these regulations that Israel was not guilty of murder because they were the instruments of God's holy judgment.

Within the evangelical community there are three major positions on the problem of war. Each is defended biblically and held by committed Christians.

The purpose of this part of the chapter is to review each position and offer the biblical defense of each. A short critique closes each section.

## Biblical Pacifism

This position is based on God's call to be Christ's disciple. The Christian is to accept the person and teachings of Jesus and follow in His footsteps, regardless of the consequences. This includes Jesus' command to love your enemies. The goal of biblical pacifism is to lead people to a saving knowledge of Jesus Christ, bringing reconciliation with God and others, and becoming ministers of the Gospel of reconciliation to everyone. This goal, the pacifist argues, cannot be attained while at the same time participating in a program of ill will, retaliation, or war.

For the pacifist, the Old Testament does not justify war any more than it does polygamy or slavery. Christ came as the fulfillment of the Law and He is God's final message. John Drescher, a defender of biblical pacifism, humorously states that the Christian cannot say:

> Love your enemies [except in wartime]; Put up the sword in its place, for all that take the sword shall perish with the sword [except when the government tells me to fight]; If a man says, "I love God," and hates his brother, he is a liar [except when he fights in a war]; Bless those who persecute you, bless and curse not [except when my country is at war].[3]

Norman Geisler writes:

> Killing is always wrong, the pacifist categorically declares. That is the point of Exodus 20:13 buttressed with Jesus' words in Matthew 5:39, "Do not resist him who is evil." The Christian is always to take the higher moral ground by protecting and securing human life. That is why war, to the pacifist, is simply mass murder, whether done within one's own society or on men in another society. Instead, Christians are to love enemies, not kill them, which is the simple point of Matthew 5:44 and Romans 12:19-21. Myron Augsburger, a stern pacifist, declares that Jesus "never sanctioned war, never approved violence." Instead, His "every word and action repudiated man's way of hate, murder, violence and self-defense...."[4]

For this reason, argues the pacifist, non-violence is a higher form of resistance; that is, violence is not the only viable option. John Stott reviews a case from World War II to illustrate:

> In his interviews with German generals after World War II, Liddell-Hart found that "violent forms of resistance had not been very effective or

troublesome to them," for they knew how to cope with these. But they had been baffled and disconcerted by the nonviolent resistance which they encountered in Denmark, Holland and Norway.[5]

War breeds more war and it means Christians will kill other Christians, a reprehensible option for Christ's disciples.

The major New Testament support for pacifism is the Sermon on the Mount. Jesus addressed people who were under oppressive foreign occupation. He did not advocate political revolution but only spiritual revolution. Jesus demanded active peacemaking—like going the extra mile—which could change the oppression and vengeful hatred into a new relationship of willful service and reconciliation. Furthermore, His life was characterized by love and nonviolence in His relationships with people and in His death. He, therefore, demonstrated the way of peace. This is powerfully illustrated in His statement: "My kingdom is not of this world. If My kingdom were of this world, then My servants would be fighting . . . but as it is, My kingdom is not of this realm" (John 18:36).

In Romans 13, Paul declares that authorities are established by God and that the believer is to be submissive to government commands as long as it does not require disobeying God's laws. If obedience to God conflicts with human authority, Christians must be willing to bear the consequences as Christ and His disciples did. Full allegiance must be to God first. The New Testament relationship between Christians and the state is to "pray for and honor always, to overthrow never, and to obey when not in conflict with God's will."[6]

Scripture lays out clearly the pacifist lifestyle. To kill a non-Christian in war would be taking away any further opportunity for that person to be saved from sin. Christians are to sacrifice their lives for their brother, not kill him. For Christians to be fighting Christians is to put Caesar, not Jesus, as Lord.[7] Believers are to love their enemies. If force is necessary, it must be imposed in such a manner that reconciliation will result. The Gospel forbids force that results in death. God's children put their faith to work by giving help to the needy and bearing one another's burdens. This is the opposite of militarism. This Christian is a peacemaker. Menno Simons argued:

> The regenerated do not go to war, nor engage in strife. They are the children of peace who have beaten their swords into plowshares and their spears into pruning hooks and know of no war. Since we are to be conformed to the image of Christ, how can we then fight our enemies with the sword? Spears and swords of iron we leave to those who, alas, consider human blood and swine's blood of well-nigh equal value.[8]

## Christian Activism

This view represents the conviction that it is always right to participate in war; it is the conviction, "my country, right or wrong." Governments are given authority to punish evil in both the Old Testament and the New Testament. Genesis 9:5-6 is the beginning of government with the authority to shed blood, presumably to deal with other nations who commit aggression and violence. Another key biblical passage for this position is Romans 13:1-7, which, for this position, argues that government is established by God and Christians must therefore submit. Verse 4 sees the ruler as a "minister" of God who "wields the sword" for justice. Since the obligation of the Christian is submission to the state and since the state has the responsibility to use force, Christians should always fight.[9] Personal feelings really play no role at all.

For the activist, government is the only guarantee of order and security. If there is no government, there will be anarchy. Thus, individuals who share the benefits of government must also share in its defense when that is necessary. It is just, according to this position, for the citizen to fulfill this obligation. Partial or total refusal to participate in defending the nation and obeying the government will further lead to anarchy and chaos. Citizens cannot, therefore, be given the freedom to choose to participate or not participate in war.

The major challenge for this view is when the state's commands contradict God's commands. When the apostles were charged by the Sanhedrin not to preach the gospel, they responded, "We must obey God rather than men" (Acts 5:29). Similarly, in the Old Testament, Shadrach, Meshach, and Abednego disobeyed an order to bow down to an idol (Daniel 3), as did Daniel when he was ordered not to pray (Daniel 6). These several biblical examples demonstrate the fallacy of the activist position. The Christian obeys government until it is a sin to obey government.

## The Just War Tradition

Pacifism and activism are the two extremes on the war issue. Pacifism says it is never right to participate in war; activism says it is always right. Through the history of the church, a mediating view has developed called the just war tradition. This tradition sees some wars as unjust and some as just. The challenge lies in discerning which wars are just.

Since the time of the fifth-century theologian Augustine, the majority of Christians have accepted the proposition that there exists a set of criteria whereby a war and its methods are deemed "just." What follows is a summary of the most widely accepted criteria for the just war tradition:

- **A Just Cause**—A just cause for the use of force exists whenever it is necessary either to repel an unjust attack, to retake something wrongly taken, or to punish evil. An example of this criterion is Saddam Hussein's invasion of Kuwait in 1990. Ethically speaking, just war theorists argue, Saddam's action was a flagrant case of aggression and therefore it was justifiable for the world community to repel his unjust aggression.

- **Right Authority**—This criterion focuses on established, legitimate, and properly constituted authority using force for a "just cause." In the United States, this "right authority" consists in the powers granted to the President of the United States by the War Powers Act or by a congressional declaration of war. In international affairs today, "right authority" might involve action by the UN Security Council authorizing the use of force. The point of this criterion focuses on legitimate authority, not private individuals who wage war.

- **Right Intention**—This criterion stresses the end goal for the use of force. The aim must be, for example, to turn back or undo aggression and then to deter such aggression in the future. The end for the use of force must be peace, not aggression or continued war. Again, the Gulf War of 1991 offers an example of this just war criterion. The world community had no aggressive aims against the territory or people of Iraq. "Right intention" in this conflict meant rolling back Saddam's aggression, establishing the peace of the Middle East, and assuring that safeguards would protect that peace in the future.

- **Proportionate Means**—As a criterion, this point centers on just means in the use of force; it must be appropriate to the goal. For example, allowing aggression to stand, this view argues, is condoning an evil in itself and opening the door to yet further evil. Therefore, military force, whether land, air, or sea forces are involved, must be proportionate to the goal. Using nuclear weapons, for example, would be disproportionate in rolling back aggression of an underdeveloped nation with no air force or navy. Using chemical and biological weapons is another example of disproportionate means.

- **Last Resort**—This criterion involves the legitimate government using all diplomatic and foreign policy resources, including economic sanctions, to force the aggressive nation to pull back. If the aggressor responds with intransigence and continued belligerence, the legitimate government has no choice but use of military force. Again, the Iraq crisis of the 1990–1991 offers a classic example of this criterion: The allies used economic sanctions, diplomatic activity, and personal diplomacy to change Saddam Hussein's aggressive actions against Kuwait. He refused. Therefore, just war advocates argue, the world community was just in rolling back his aggressive actions.

• **Noncombatant Immunity**—This is the most difficult criterion for the just war position. The military force used must be discriminant—the moral principle that seeks to protect noncombatants in war by prohibiting their being used directly or intentionally targeted by military force. Of course this means going to all ends not to intentionally attack civilians, not to bomb civilian neighborhoods, and not to kill intentionally and indiscriminately the civilian population of an enemy.

With the advent of weapons of mass destruction, whether nuclear or chemical or biological, one sees how difficult this criterion becomes for modern warfare. Noncombatant immunity does not exist. Because entire populations are decimated, neither does proportionate means. This is why many Christians argue that nuclear warfare does not meet this just war criterion and is therefore immoral and a sin.[10]

In summary, the just war position argues that war must be fought only for a just cause and not to pursue aggrandizement, glory, or vengeance. War must be declared by a legitimate authority and have a reasonable chance of success. The resulting good must outweigh the evil of warfare and of allowing the wrongdoing that provokes the war to continue. War must be a last resort after less violent approaches have failed. Civilian populations must not be deliberately attacked, every effort must be made to minimize casualties among them, and no unnecessary force must be wielded against either troops or civilians.

Those who support this tradition give the following biblical passages as support:

• Genesis 9:6—Here we find part of the Noahic covenant where God delineates the responsibility of humans to be instruments of His justice. With the killing of humans comes the responsibility of holding the murderer accountable. This, by inference, is what nations must do as well—hold aggressors and perpetrators of international violence accountable-even if it means using military force.

• Matthew 22:21; 1 Timothy 2:1,2; Titus 3:1; 1 Peter 2:13—In these passages, Christians are called upon to practice civil obedience to properly constituted authority. As stated earlier in this chapter, this is not blind obedience, for when human law conflicts with God's law, the Christian obeys God.

- Romans 13:4—In this classic passage, God delegates to the state the responsibility to use the sword as an instrument of justice and to punish evil. By extension, this tradition holds nations must use military force to promote justice and punish evil.

- John 18:11; Luke 22:36—In these passages Jesus deals with the use of the sword as an instrument of self-defense. In the first He rebukes Peter for his misuse of the sword; He does not condemn the use of the sword in self-defense. In the Luke passage, Jesus seems to be allowing for a legitimate use of the sword for self-defense when, in light of His rejection, He instructs His disciples: "Whoever has no sword is to sell his coat and buy one." Again, by inference, nations acting in self-defense are justified in using military force.

There is enormous tension in thinking about the just war tradition. Yet, because we live in a sin-cursed world, it is probably the wisest choice among the three major options. But it should never soothe or bring comfort! Thinking about this tradition and then its implementation should always vex and trouble. If a nation fights what it has determined to be a just war, it must never do so with arrogance and bombastic pride; instead, it must fight with tears and with agonizing tension. War should never be easy. It remains one of the most perplexing ethical issues for the Christian.

## Capital Punishment

As with the issue of war, capital punishment is filled with intellectual and theological tension. This section does not deal with how capital punishment is practiced in the United States or any other country. Instead, the focus is the issue of capital punishment and whether one can make a biblical defense of it as a responsibility of the state. If humans bear God's image (Genesis 1:26-27), then taking the life of an image-bearer in a premeditated act of murder ethically demands just punishment. Killing a human being is an attack on the Creator God. It is a rejection of His sovereignty over human life (Deuteronomy 32:39). But is it just to make the punishment capital? This section will argue yes.

There are several key biblical passages that make the case for capital punishment as a just obligation of the state:

- Genesis 9:6—As Noah exits the ark, God establishes a new relationship with the human race and a new code on which to base human relationships. Because of the flood's destruction of all life, future generations might conclude that life is cheap to God and assume that humans can do likewise. However, the covenant affirms the sacredness of human life and that murder is punishable by losing one's life. The text, therefore, institutes the principle of talionic justice, or law of like punishment. It is not a harsh principle of justice, for it establishes the premise that the punishment should fit the crime. It is summarized elsewhere in God's Word as "eye for eye, tooth for tooth" (Exodus 21:23-25). The point of this covenant with Noah is that God removed justice from the deceased family's hands and placed it in the hands of human government, eliminating the personal revenge factor and emotional anger.

- The Mosaic Law—God's moral law revealed to Moses was not the first time God delegated the authority of capital punishment. It is central to Genesis 9:6 and is clearly implied in Genesis 4 in His dialogue with Cain (vv. 10, 14). What God did with the Mosaic Law was broaden the responsibility to include many other offenses: murder (Exodus 21:12; Numbers 35:16-31); working on the Sabbath (Exodus 35:2); cursing father and mother (Leviticus 20:9); adultery (Leviticus 20:10); incest (Leviticus 20:11-12); sodomy (Leviticus 20:13, 15-16); false prophesying (Deuteronomy 13:1-10, 18:20); idolatry (Exodus 20:4); rape (Deuteronomy 22:25); keeping an ox that has killed a human being (Exodus 21:29); kidnapping (Exodus 21:16); and intrusion of an alien into a sacred place (Numbers 1:51, 3:10, 38). The form of execution was normally stoning or burning.[11]

- Romans 13:1-7—Verse 4 is the key verse in this critical section on the authority of the state in our lives. It gives the state the authority to wield the "sword" in its role as the punisher of evil: "It [the civil ruler] does not bear the sword for nothing; for it is a minister of God, an avenger who brings wrath upon the one who practices evil." The word used for sword here is *machaira*, which refers not only to a sword used in battle, but also to a sword used in executions, as when Herod killed James, the brother of John, in Acts 12:1-2.[12] Paul's use of this word gives strong support to the state receiving from God the authority to execute. It gives no help in deciding which crimes are punishable by capital punishment.

In summary, the principle of talionic justice, implied in Genesis 4:10, 14, was clearly instituted in Genesis 9:6 and reaffirmed quite broadly in the Mosaic Law. It is likewise power delegated to the state according to Romans 13:4. The New Testament did not negate the Old Testament standard of capital punishment. The continuity of the Testaments is affirmed.

**Is Capital Punishment a Deterrent?**

Both the criminal justice system and theologians are divided as to whether capital punishment deters criminal behavior. When comparing crime rates of states that use capital punishment to those that do not, it is impossible to argue that capital punishment is a deterrent. Statistics can be stated to posit whatever you want them to say. But, from the perspective of Scripture, this is beside the point.

The view of capital punishment defended in this chapter gives focus to the fundamental biblical reason for capital punishment. Specifically, killing another human (an image-bearer of God) demands taking the murderer's life based on the principle of talionic justice. Whether this form of justice deters further murders is almost irrelevant to the issue. Justice demands payment. The universal and binding principle that God instituted in Genesis 9:6 is as applicable today as it was in Noah's day.

In conclusion, whether one is thinking about war or about capital punishment, there exists enormous tension. Neither issue is simple; each is intensely difficult. This chapter has suggested the just war tradition as a possible way of reducing some of the tension on the issue of war. It has also defended the matter of capital punishment as an issue of justice. Both war and capital punishment are carried out with remorse and tears, looking to God for wisdom and discernment.

## For Further Discussion

1. Explain the use of the term "kill" in Exodus 20:13.

2. Summarize in one sentence the three views on the matter of war:

   • Pacifism

   • Activism

   • Just War

3. Summarize in detail the biblical passages used to defend pacifism and activism.

4. List and explain the criteria used to defend the just war tradition.

5. Summarize in detail the biblical defense of the just war tradition.

6. Explain how each of the following was used in the defense of the biblical principle of capital punishment:

   • Genesis 4:10, 14

- Genesis 9:6
- Talionic justice
- Romans 13:4

7. In the author's opinion how important is the issue of deterrence to the question of capital punishment?

## Notes

[1] Peter Craigie, *The Problem of War in the Old Testament* (Grand Rapids: Zondervan, 1978), 58.

[2] Charles Ryrie, *You Mean the Bible Teaches That . . .* (Chicago: Moody, 1974), 30.

[3] John Drescher, "Why Christians Shouldn't Carry Swords," *Christianity Today*, November 7, 1984, 17.

[4] Norman Geisler, *Christian Ethics: Options and Issues* (Grand Rapids, MI: Baker, 1989), 223.

[5] John Stott, *Involvements* (Grand Rapids, MI: Zondervan, 1985), 44.

[6] Drescher, 23.

[7] Ibid., 21-22.

[8] Quoted in Jurgen Luas, "Charismatic or Military Power?" *Christianity Today*, November 30, 1983, 112.

[9] Giesler, 225.

[10] Ibid., 220-228.

[11] Ryrie, 26-27.

[12] John Eidsmoe, *God and Caesar* (Wheaton: Crossway, 1989), 200.

# The Ethics of Work
# and Race
# 10

Some people hate to do it. Some love to do it. Some go to great lengths to avoid doing it. Some do it too much. While there are many different attitudes toward work, one thing remains constant: Work must be done. Since the garden of Eden, everyone has worked or depended on someone else's work for their survival. Furthermore, work sets a person's lifestyle—where to live, when to sleep and eat, time with family, and even dress. If a person is not content with work, the rest of life is in turmoil.

What should be the Christian's attitude toward work? Is it a blessing or a curse? Is work a means to justify the ends of leisure and entertainment? This chapter focuses on developing the Christian work ethic and discussing the proper perspective on work relationships.

## A Biblical View of Work

Work is ordained by God. It was His creative invention from the beginning. While we do not usually think of God as working and while we do not know all the details, the Bible declares that God worked (Genesis 1–2). By working we resemble God. Like God, humans have the ability to work, make plans, implement them, and be creative. In addition, Genesis 1:28 and 2:15 proclaim that God gave humans the task of ruling over and taking care of His creation. Carl Henry writes:

> Through his work, man shares the creation purpose of God in subduing nature, whether he is a miner with dirty hands, a mechanic with a greasy face, or a stenographer with stencil smudged fingers. Work is permeated by purpose; it is intended to serve God, benefit mankind, make nature subservient to the moral program for creation. Man must therefore apply his whole being—heart and mind, as well as hand—to the daily job. As God's fellow worker he is to reflect God's creative ability on Monday in the factory no less than on Sunday when commemorating the day of rest and worship.[1]

Apparently Adam and Eve's pre-fall work had both a physical and spiritual dimension. With respect to their work in the garden of Eden, God told them "to cultivate it and keep it" (Genesis 2:15). The Hebrew word translated "keep" is used in 3:24 referring to the angel who was "to guard the way to the tree of life." Adam and Eve had that same responsibility, an immense spiritual stewardship, before their rebellion against God. Therefore, work has both a physical and a spiritual dimension.

Work is not only toilsome, due to sin, but it is for a lifetime. Genesis 3:19 says, "By the sweat of your face you will eat bread, till *you return to the ground*" (emphasis added). Apparently God intends that humans are to work as long as they live. Meaningful activity plays a critical role in being a human being: Retirement does not end work; rather, it must include work for a person's overall well-being. This proposition speaks volumes about the manner in which Western civilization views the retirement years. The magical age of 65 should not end meaningful, purposeful work.

When interpreting Genesis 3:17-19, some argue that work is a curse resulting from the fall. While God's curse in these verses has enormous effect on work, work itself is not a punishment. God's point is that there pain and toil are involved when humans seek productive results. There are likewise counteracting forces that tend to restrict those results. Until death, humans are always faced with painful, laborious toil. God did not create work as drudgery; that is the result of sin. Therefore, we speak today of "getting back to the grind" or to the "salt mine." Work today is tedious, difficult, and often frustrating.

Despite the "painful toil," work has three basic purposes: to meet human needs, to provide for a quality of life, and to serve (and worship) God. First, work provides money (or resources) to supply the necessities of life. Jesus said that it is proper to pray for our "daily bread" (Matthew 6:11) and a manner in which that prayer is answered is through work. Second, work enhances the quality of life. Work enhances the satisfaction of life and is the strongest predictor of life span, even above general happiness and other physical factors.[2]

Furthermore, psychological and mental health are related to work. A person receives a sense of personal dignity and worth from work. Most Americans, when introducing themselves, share their name and occupation. People who are without work often suffer from depression, poor self image, and other mental illnesses.[3] God gave work as a gift of fulfillment to life. The human is to enjoy it for more than simply its economic benefits. Ecclesiastes 2:24-25 (NIV) argues that a human being "can do nothing better than . . . find satisfaction in his work. This too, I see, is from the hand of God, for without him, who can eat or find enjoyment?"

The final purpose of work is to serve God. Colossians 3:22–4:1 is the major biblical passage on the proper ethical attitude for work. Here Paul writes to slaves and masters. However, remember that the vast majority of workers in the Roman empire were slaves, working usually for life with limited rights. In many ways, the slave's relationship to his master is similar to the employee/employer relationship of today.

In this passage, the Apostle Paul details three principles on the ethic of work. First is the principle of obedience, consistency, and sincerity (Colossians 3:22). The Christian is to approach work as a matter of obedience to God; it is a stewardship from Him that demands a commitment of obedience and a consistency, even when the boss is not looking. Christian workers likewise approach the job sincerely, in a conscientious manner. The second principle is the lordship of Jesus Christ; Christian workers serve "the Lord Christ" (Colossians 3:23-24). One could easily argue that our real boss is Jesus Christ. We work for Him and we are to see our work as service to Him, not simply our employer. Finally, verse 24 states that the reason Christians maintain such a high work ethic is because we know God will reward us. In other words, there is eternal significance to work. Part of God's reward system involves reward for our work. What would happen to the quality of products and to productivity if all workers viewed work according to the standards of Colossians 3?

From this chapter so far, it would seem that people should be more excited about the idea of going to work. Yet the opposite is true. Strikes, low productivity, union demands, absenteeism, and high turnover rates are symptoms of dissatisfied workers. Due to sin, the meaning of work has become distorted and twisted. Work today is but a means to an end. The goal is to enjoy the end product and work only because it is a means to that end—leisure. Even Christians fall into this mind-set. Leisure is not the end. Work, as this chapter has shown, is the end in itself. It is a stewardship from God, and how we approach it has eternal implications.

## Implications of the Christian Work Ethic

From the argument presented in this chapter, it is possible to deduce several implications for the Christian work ethic:

- **Everyone should work.** Since God ordained work, humans will only find fulfillment in working. It is the key to finding purpose in life.

- **Excellence is the worker's standard.** Ephesians 6:6-7 exhorts the Christian to "render service, as to the Lord, and not to men," not to be men-pleasers but God-pleasers. God's standard of excellence needs to be the human standard.

- **Respect and obedience are to be observed at work.** Both Colossians and Ephesians challenge the slave (employee) to show respect to his master (employer). The master (employer) is likewise to show respect and treat kindly his slave (employee). Love, mutual respect, and justice must characterize the employer/employee relationship.

- **All professions and all kinds of work, assuming they are legal and biblically ethical, are honorable before the Lord.** There simply is no dichotomy between sacred and secular work. All work brings glory to God and fulfillment to the human, if it is done to God's glory (1 Corinthians 10:31).

- **Work provides an opportunity for a witness.** As the disciple of Christ follows the Christian work ethic, he or she manifests a powerful message, both verbal and non-verbal, of a supernatural approach to work. The world today needs this powerful witness.

- **Work is actually a form of worship.** Such an attitude cultivates honesty, integrity, and excellence.

In conclusion, the Gospel of Jesus Christ brings total transformation to the human being. It brings personal responsibility, dignity, and purpose—core values for a productive, God-centered work ethic. The Christian's daily job is a daily offering to God. It is a transformational, supernatural, eternally significant perspective about the mundane chore called work.

## The Ethics of Race

America has a history littered with ugly manifestations of the sin of racism. Principally, the United States institutionalized chattel slavery that was fundamentally racist in its orientation; it centered on the enslavement of Africans. It took a bitter and costly Civil War (1861–1865) to destroy this monstrous evil. Today, almost fifty years have passed since the Civil Rights Acts of 1964 and 1965 which freed African-Americans from legalized segregation, denial of voting rights, and blanket discrimination in the labor market. Racial identification, of any kind, no longer presents a hindrance to voting privilege. In 2008, the United States voters even elected the first African-American President, Barak Obama. Although minorities (particularly African-American) are far from economic parity with Causasians, yet high positions in government, the military, business, and education are attainable.

Nevertheless, almost everyone agrees that something remains wrong and the dream of Martin Luther King, Jr., for an integrated society where people would be judged by character rather than color has not been fully realized. Racism, in all its ugliness, remains a part of American civilization. What does God's Word say about race? How should we view people of different color? What is the biblical solution to the ongoing remnants of racism toward all minorities in America?

There are several biblical passages critical to forming Christmindedness on the subject of race:

- 1 Corinthians 1:18—The Apostle Paul establishes that from God's viewpoint there are only two groups of human beings: those who are with Christ and those who are without Christ; in other words, those who have trusted Jesus Christ as Savior and those who have not. The Bible does not allow for racial differences as a basis for discrimination or ranking of humans. Jesus' death on Calvary's cross was for all of humanity: red, black, brown, yellow, and white.

- Genesis 9:20-27—Historically, this passage has been used to justify the enslavement of the black race that occurred in the United States after 1619. Since some of Ham's descendants populated Africa, Noah's curse (some conclude) must therefore apply to all those who are from Africa. Many in the southern part of the United States prior to the Civil War used this argument to justify racial slavery. Unfortunately this perception about Noah's curse remains today.

 The behavior of Noah after the flood provided the occasion for Ham's sin. There is a remarkable contrast between Noah's conduct before the flood and after. Noah, who walked in righteousness with God, planted a vineyard, became drunk, and lay naked in his tent. Unfortunately, the Bible never approves of drunkenness or nakedness. Neither will  bring true joy; rather, they are the origin of personal slavery and decadence!

 Noah's actions induce Ham's sin. Verse 22 states that Ham "saw the nakedness of his father, and told his two brothers." Despite many interpretations, there is no clear evidence that Ham did anything other than see his father's nakedness. As Allen Ross makes clear, "Nakedness in the Old Testament was from the beginning a thing of shame for fallen humankind. For Adam and Eve as sinners, the state of nakedness was both undignified and vulnerable. . . .To be exposed meant to be unprotected; to see someone uncovered was to bring dishonor and to gain advantage for potential exploitation."[4] By stressing that Ham entered and saw Noah's nakedness, Genesis depicts Ham's looking as a moral flaw, a first step in the abandonment of a moral code. In the words of Ross, "Ham desecrated a natural and sacred barrier. His going to tell his brothers about it without covering the old man aggravated the act."[5]

But Noah's curse in verses 25-27 was on Ham's youngest son, Canaan, that Canaan would be a "servant of servants" (i.e., slavery). Noah's curse anticipated in Canaan the evil traits that marked his father Ham and so judged him. The text prepares the reader by twice mentioning that Ham was Canaan's father, signifying more than lineage. To the Hebrew mind, the Canaanites were the most natural embodiment of Ham. "Everything the Canaanites did in their pagan existence was symbolized by the attitude of Ham. From the moment the patriarchs entered the land, these tribes were their corrupting influence."[6] The constant references to "nakedness" and "uncovering" in Leviticus 18 designate a people enslaved sexually, reminding Israel of the sin of Ham. These descendants of Ham were not cursed because of what Ham did; they were cursed because they acted as their ancestor did.[7]

In conclusion, it is simply impossible to see any justification for slavery or any other aspect of inferiority from the curse on Canaan. It is a gross distortion of God's Word to do so. Furthermore, as Charles Ryrie affirms, "it is [also] irrelevant today since it would be difficult, if not impossible, to identify a Canaanite."[8]

Acts 10:34-35—The point of this extraordinary passage is that the salvation God offers is to all humans everywhere, regardless of racial background or characteristics. Peter learns that ". . . God does not show favoritism but accepts men from every nation who fear him and do what is right" (NIV). Racial hatred or discrimination is impossible when one sees people the way God does.

• James 2:1-9—The story is told of Mahatma Gandhi's search for truth and harmony for his people of India. Raised a Hindu, Gandhi did not believe that Hinduism offered the solution to the horrendous discrimination and rigid caste system of India. As he studied law in South Africa, he believed that Christianity might offer the solution to India's problems. Hoping to find in Christianity what Hinduism lacked, he attended a church in South Africa. Because the South African church embraced the system of racial segregation called apartheid, the usher offered him a seat on the floor. Gandhi demurred, that he might as well remain a Hindu, for Christianity has its own caste system as well. What a tragedy!

James 2 will have none of this. James decries the typical situation of the early church where the wealthy were given a place of privilege and honor in worship, while the poor were only permitted to sit on the floor. Such discriminatory practices violate God's royal law, "Love your neighbor as yourself." To show favoritism is sin; it desecrates God's standard of love.

The church of Jesus Christ should therefore model the supernatural impartiality that refuses to discriminate. The church should model reconciliation of all races and ethnic groups. It should cut the radical path for all of society, for it alone sees people the way God sees them: Whatever race or ethnic background, all need Jesus Christ and all bear His image. The church has the radical solution to society's struggle with racial and ethnic differences. It is a supernatural solution: disciples of Jesus Christ who have experienced His salvation and who love one another with the supernatural love of their Savior. All the world needs to see this radical solution lived out in the church.

## For Further Discussion

1. Show from Scripture that work predated the fall of Adam and Eve into sin.

2. In what sense does work have a spiritual dimension? Explain.

3. What does the author argue are the three purposes for work?

4. From Colossians 3:21–4:1, summarize the Apostle Paul's three principles for work.

5. List and describe the author's six implications of the Christian work ethic.

6. Using the following Scripture passages, show that racism is a sin:
   - 1 Corinthians 1:18
   - Acts 10:34-35
   - James 2:1-9

7. How would you respond to someone who says the "curse of Ham" mentioned in Genesis 9 proves that black enslavement was part of God's plan? Be sure to focus on a proper understanding of Genesis 9:20-27.

# Notes

[1] Quoted in John A. Bernabaum and Simon A. Steer, *Why Work?* (Grand Rapids, MI: Baker, 1986), 6-7.

[2] See Arthur Holmes, *Contours of a World View* (Grand Rapids, MI: Eerdmans, 1983), 219, and Stanley Cramer and Edwin L. Herr, *Career Guidance and Counseling Through the Life Span* (Boston: Little Brown, 1979), 387.

[3] Holmes, 216.

[4] Alan Ross, Jr. *Creation and Blessing* (Grand Rapids, MI: Baker, 1988), 215.

[5] Ibid.

[6] Ibid., 217.

[7] Ibid., 218.

[8] Charles Ryrie, *You Mean the Bible Teaches That . . .* (Chicago: Moody, 1974), 60.

# The Christian, the Arts, and Entertainment
# 11

Today, the arts—both performing and visual—are often ignored by the church of Jesus Christ. Rarely do you have evangelical Christians attending art museums, classical music concerts, or ballet. Such enterprises are often considered secular and unworthy of Christian involvement. The result is that the arts are almost exclusively in the domain of the world; very few Christians are in leadership positions of the arts, nor do they regularly participate in the visual or performing arts. This is a tragedy, for God is a God of beauty and He desires that His creatures reflect His commitment to beauty as well. That is certainly part of being in the image of God.

Several decades ago, Franky Schaeffer, in a highly provocative book, *Addicted to Mediocrity*, argued that Christians have sacrificed the artistic prominence they enjoyed for centuries and instead have settled for mediocrity: "Christian" doodads, trinkets, T-shirts and bumper stickers are the only major contribution Christians today make to creative expression. This is a sad state of affairs and should not be. This chapter presents a clear, biblical argument that Christians need to be involved in the arts. To neglect this area of culture is to surrender a pivotal sphere once dominated by Christians (e.g., the medieval cathedrals, northern Renaissance and Reformation painting, etc.).

## Creativity: A Christian Concept

When the Christian thinks of creativity, it is usually in the context of the arts. Those with artistic ability are said to be "creative types," while the untalented look on with envy. But this is totally unbiblical, for creativity is basic to life. God is a God of beauty, creativity, and variety; one only need look at His physical creation! Because we bear His image (Genesis 1:26), creativity is a part of being in the image of God. Indeed, in his marvelous book, *Culture Making: Recovering Our Creative Calling*, Andy Crouch contends that, in the biblical creation narrative, Adam and Eve are presented as "creative cultivators," who are to make something out of their world.[1] God trusted them to cultivate the garden of Eden and gave them enormous creative freedom to do so. That primary stewardship has not been altered or erased because of sin. As Christians who seek to do all for God's glory (1 Corinthians 10:31), we are creative cultivators of our world; we seek to make something out of the culture in which God places us. Whether decorating an apartment or home, caring for our lawn, painting a picture, taking photographs, or anything that involves personal expression, we are to be creative cultivators of God's world. This is both a challenging and a liberating way for believers to live. As image-bearers of the living God, there are no limits to our expressive creativity.

## A Definition of Creativity

Peter Angeles defines "creation" as "bringing something new into existence out of something previously existing."[2] The noun, "creation," refers to the act of creation or the product of the act. The adjective, "creative," refers to the quality one possesses to create. The verb is transitive, meaning to produce, to give rise to something.

Several conclusions flow from this definition: (1) Creativity is not quantitative but qualitative. (2) Creativity is a process that involves movement, progression, and change. There is no single creative act, only creative action. Painting a picture involves many acts; taken as a whole, painting is a process. (3) Because creativity is a quality and a process, it cannot be measured. The only way to "see" creativity is through its effects (e.g., paintings, compositions, sculptures, etc.). (4) Because "create" is a transitive verb, it always has an object. Thus, the creative process always has a product. The composer produces a composition, the painter a painting, and the sculptor a sculpture. The product of God's creative work in Genesis 1:1 is the universe. (5) Finally, creativity is an actualizing of potential. Things that exist have the potential to be rearranged, put together, or simply become different.

## Biblical Principles of Creativity

Rooted in the proposition that God is the Creator and we are His creatures, the following principles provide the basis for thinking and acting biblically when it comes to creativity. Such a foundation, then, enables Christians to be creative cultivators of God's world.

- **Human creativity derives its value from God's creativity.** In Genesis 1:26-30, after God had finished His creative work, He detailed His creation mandate for humanity: Humans are to subdue and have dominion over His creation. When we exercise that dominion status, we are exercising the creativity He entrusted to us.

- **Human creativity manifests God's image.** Bearing God's image means at least that we resemble Him. Creative imagination is vested in the physical world, along with the human capacity for sensory, intellectual and emotional delight, and pleasure. Because God is creative, we carry that same capacity as His creatures.

- **Creativity is a capacity to be developed in all persons, not just a creative elite.** All humans have some creative potential. Since all bear His image, all have some dimension of creativity.

- **Creativity extends to all cultural activities, including art, science, work, play, thought, and action.** One of the clear teachings of God's Word is the Lordship of Jesus Christ. If He is Lord of all, then that Lordship extends to all dimensions of life; there are no exceptions. Since we have dominion status over His creation, we exercise that dominion in a creative way, and there are no exceptions to that either.

- **Human creativity exists for the glory of God.** As 1 Corinthians 10:31 makes clear, we are to do all to the glory of God. Each time we exercise our creative potential, we are giving glory to the One who created and gifted us. [3]

## Characteristics of the Creative Christian

What follows is a suggested list of characteristics that foster creativity. It is not exhaustive, merely suggestive. It is rooted in the proposition that as God is creative, so are His image-bearers.

- **The creative person is well-rounded.** This means that one does not exercise creativity in only a single area of life but in all areas, including the social, intellectual, spiritual, and psychological dimensions of life. In a word, the mature, growing Christian is a balanced person who gives focus to the creative development of all dimensions of life.

- **The creative person is curious.** Curiosity is an inquisitiveness about something, an eagerness to learn and grow. When we realize that all aspects of creation are God's, then our goal is to understand *all* of God's creation. Our curiosity to learn and inquire produces creativity.

- **The creative person is courageous.** It takes courage to learn a new subject, to explore a new area of knowledge, or to do an activity never attempted before (e.g., painting, music, ballet). To be bold and courageous goes hand in hand with creativity.

• **The creative person is humble.** The realization of absolute dependence on God is the beginning of creativity. Whatever we have in terms of gifts or talents comes from God, and we exercise those for His glory (1 Corinthians 10:31). Humility and a proper understanding of self are the keys to the proper exercise of God's gifts.

## What Inhibits Creative Potential?

One of the greatest killers of creative potential is the "screen"—television, the computer screen, smartphones, iPads, etc. Consider television: According to Richard Zoglin, "except for school and family, no institution plays a bigger role in shaping the American child" than television.[4] The average American child will watch five thousand hours of television by first grade and will have watched a total of nineteen thousand hours by high school graduation. The lifetime total for television viewing is nine years by the age of sixty-five.[5] The average home today has the TV on six hours and seventeen minutes a day!

The effect on the brain of watching television is staggering. Clement Walchshauser observes that "watching television produces highly altered brain wave states when people watch for a mere twenty minutes." It puts the brain into a totally passive condition unaware of its surroundings and lessening the attention span.[6] In addition, obsessive television watching has further negative effects:

• **It demands our time.** It is nearly addictive as it draws the viewer in, resulting in more and more time spent in front of the TV and less serving God, family, or others.

• **It determines behavior.** A national report titled *Television and Behavior* was issued by the National Institute of Health in 1982. A summary of more than 2,500 studies conducted since 1972, the report demonstrated that there is "overwhelming evidence of a causal link between children's watching television violence and their performance of violent acts."[7]

• **It distorts the perception of reality.** Children, especially, confuse real life with TV life and tend to adopt TV's values. A recent study discovered that 90 percent of boys surveyed would rather watch their favorite TV program than spend time with their fathers. Quentin Schultze reports that "...the lure of the television is strong for young boys, who especially like the aggressive characters and automobile violence of the action shows."[8]

- **It dulls moral sensitivity.** A steady diet of soap operas, situation comedies, or movies desensitizes and enables one to accept that which not too many years earlier would have been rejected. Adultery, premarital sex, homosexuality, murder, and violent rage are all a part of entertainment today. Obsessive viewing of such activities produces an acceptance and toleration of acts repugnant to God.

- **It destroys meaningful family life.** When a family spends its time in front of the television, there is no significant communication occurring, nor is there time for games, reading, music, etc. It is lethal to creativity and enjoying family relationships.

But we must consider the "screen" more broadly than TV. Recently, the American Academy of Pediatrics (AAP), expressed deep concern about the effects of exposure to "screens" (i.e., TV screens, computer screens, monitors, iPads, smartphones, and other such devices) on children. In fact, the AAP called upon parents to place severe limits on the exposure of young children to such "screens." According to the AAP, 90 percent of parents reported that their children under the age of two "watch some form of electronic media." These children, parents also reported, watch an average of one to two hours of TV a day. The report also contends that a considerable number of parents indicated that TV "is very important for healthy development," and therefore leave the TV on virtually all waking hours. The doctors of AAP reject such a notion, arguing instead that "unstructured play and face time with parents produce far greater educational outcomes." Indeed, Benedict Carey, reporter for the *New York Times*, indicates that the AAP "makes clear that there is no such thing as an educational program [on TV] for such young children."[9] Here are some of the other findings from this report:

- TV exposure around bedtime is associated with "poor sleep habits and irregular sleep schedules, which can adversely affect mood, behavior, and learning."

- By age three, almost one-third of all children have a TV in their bedroom.

- About one year ago, the AAP argued that children and adolescents "spend more time engaged in various media than they do in any other activity except for sleeping."

- The 2010 Kaiser Foundation report suggested that children and teenagers spend more than seven hours each day engaged with various media. As noted above, that means that such individuals will have spent seven to ten years of their lives watching TV and other media.

- The number of American homes with TVs outnumbers the number of homes with indoor plumbing. The average American home with children has four TVs, one DVR, up to three DVD players, two CD players, two radios, two computers, and two video game units.

- About 70 percent of American teenagers have a TV in their bedroom and at least one-third of the nation's teenagers have a computer with Internet access in their bedroom.

- As Albert Mohler reports, "The pediatricians warned that the presence of a TV in a teenager's room is associated with higher rates of substance abuse and sexual activity." [10]

As anyone in teen ministry knows, we are in the midst of one of the greatest communication revolutions in human history—the Digital Revolution. As this chapter has shown, there is now considerable evidence about the threats this revolution poses, but it also has enormous opportunities. The key is balancing the two.

First, let's place this revolution in historical context. There have been three great communications revolutions in human history: (1) the printing revolution, ignited by Johannes Gutenberg, who developed moveable type in the mid-1450s; (2) radio, television, and movies, which transformed the communication of information and of entertainment; (3) the Digital Revolution. The Internet, digital appliances, and new modes of communication and technologies are transforming how we live and how we communicate.

Digital networks, social networks, and Internet blogs are not only communicating information, they also are shaping public opinion. Theologian Albert Mohler argues that "the digital world flattens hierarchies. A teenager might be writing that blog that scoops a major network on a major story. The great challenge for most of us is not access (the challenge of the old media) but adequate filtering. The digital world is all about open communication—the gatekeepers of old media are no longer in control." [11]

One of the most astonishing developments of this Digital Revolution is the new social media, especially Facebook. There are more than 350 million registered users of Facebook, a population larger than most nations on earth. Further, Twitter, a micro-blogging phenomenon, is now a major platform for instant news and analysis. Such aspects of the Digital Revolution are transforming how we communicate and get information, thereby changing daily routines, habits of living, and revolutionizing each aspect of life.

Second, scientists are beginning to document the effects of the Digital Revolution on the brain, especially the ability of the brain to concentrate and focus.

Theologian Albert Mohler also writes that "they have identified a physiological reward for digital stimulation—a 'dopamine squirt.' That little squirt of dopamine in the brain serves as a physiological pay-off for digital stimulation, and it can be habit-forming."[12] For teens and adults, digital games, video games, and digital gadgets become habit-forming and create what is in effect an unhealthy dependency. Indeed, a research study summary by Matt Richtel of the *New York Times* reports that Americans in 2008 consumed three times more daily information than in 1960. Those who use computers at work change windows or screens an average of 37 times an hour. Richtel also found that multitasking actually takes quite a toll on the brain's ability to concentrate on anything, including personal, one-on-one conversation.[13] Mohler argues that "the research indicates that people who are highly invested in digital involvements are less empathetic, less attentive, less patient, and less able to remember something as basic as a conversation."[14] In short, when it comes to managing personally the Digital Revolution, there is a need for balance. It is not an evil! Digital gadgets (e.g., Blackberry, iPhone, iPad.) can be wonderful tools to manage time more wisely and make us more efficient and effective. Church leaders should challenge believers to be good stewards of these tools by setting clear, discernible boundaries for themselves.

Third, are there opportunities for effective ministry using the tools of the Digital Revolution? Ed Stetzer of LifeWay Research sees four potential positives for the church when it comes to social media (e.g., Facebook, Twitter): (1) Social media can assist in community. While social media cannot replace real-life relationships, they can assist in building real community by connecting people in ways that allow them to share both the big and small things of life. Web services (e.g., Facebook) permit people who might see one another only during church on Sunday or midweek in smaller community groups to continue to share aspects of life they would not otherwise share. A network like Facebook could actually enhance encouragement or exhortation! (2) Social media can assist in communication. Email blasts, Twitter or even texting can enhance a ministry's ability to communicate effectively and efficiently. Prayer requests can be almost instantly passed on and then easily forwarded to others. In fact, a prayer network can grow almost exponentially through digital communication. (3) Social media can assist in inspiration. Twitter, Facebook, or podcasts can further enhance personal devotion time or even deeper theological investigation. Such mediums can serve as a means of introducing participants to theologians, pastors, writers, musicians, books, conferences, events, etc. Twitter, which at first seems to promote superficiality, can actually be a vehicle for theological depth and insight. (4) Social networking can actually promote more transparent introductions of people. For example, from something like Facebook we can learn much about the work of the Gospel in a person's life and how it has influenced his/her thinking, family, work, etc.[15]

For all these reasons, Stetzer reaches this compelling conclusion:

> As I consider social media in the 21st century, I cannot help but think of the spread of the gospel and the church's growth in the first century. Communication was greatly aided then by the common language of Koine Greek. Since the New Testament was written in a language accessible to so many, the Word of God was able to penetrate different cultures rapidly. Perhaps today the new media will be the 'common language' for the masses to hear the gospel.[16]

The Digital Revolution can either be a curse or a blessing. For this revolution to be a blessing, we must help believers achieve a God-honoring balance in their lives, and we must help the church view it as a tool for building the kingdom of God.

Obsessive viewing of television or the use of any "screen," then, not only affects creative potential, it likewise produces significant negative behavioral effects. It is next to impossible to see addictive television viewing or addictive video game playing as anything but harmful and potentially destructive. There is a clear need for some guidelines, rooted in Scripture, to help make wise decisions. Several of those guiding principles include:

- **The principle of stewardship of time** (Ephesians 5:15-16). Time is like any other commodity: We must decide how we will use it. This includes entertainment choices and the amount of time those choices require.

- **The principle of self-control** (1 Corinthians 6:12). One of the fruits of the Spirit is self-control (Galatians 5:23). There is no greater test of this virtue than personal discipline in the amount of time devoted to the "screen." Knowing what we know about the effects, this is the only wise choice.

- **The principle of moral purity** (Philippians 4:8). We must choose what we allow into our mind. God desires that we dwell on what is true, honorable, right, pure, lovely, of good repute, excellence and worthy of praise. These virtues produce godly living and form the grid through which we make entertainment choices. A steady diet of the "screen" in all its variations obviously violates these virtues.

- **The principle of edification** (1 Corinthians 10:23). The believer in Jesus Christ has great freedom, but with that freedom comes immense responsibility. Although we may have the freedom to participate in many forms of entertainment, most of those forms may not edify or build us up in the Christian faith. In fact, a regular diet of such entertainment may actually tear down our faith.

- **The principle of God's glory** (1 Corinthians 10:31). Most chapters in this book have focused on this overarching theme—that we do all for God's glory. There are no exceptions, including entertainment choices.

What then should Christians do? Entertainment choices are never easy, but in light of the above principles, allow me to suggest several practical suggestions for wise decision-making on entertainment:

- **Participate actively in entertainment choices.** Always ask yourself, "How is this affecting me?" In short, be a critical thinker when it comes to entertainment. Passivity will simply not cut it!

- **Be creative in choosing family entertainment.** The television or the movie theater are not the only choices. Consider a visit to an art museum, to a concert, or to a historical place. Also, consider family reading times, where you read a book out loud together. Limit the amount of time children spend in front of the computer or playing video games. Starting when the children are young makes it much easier when they reach the teen years.

- **Read carefully and critically program descriptions for video games, television programs, and movies.** Prepare your children for what they will see or do and then discuss the entertainment content, themes, and worldview presented in the program, movie, or game.

- **Keep a log of how much money the family spends on entertainment.** Periodically evaluate with the children whether too much is being spent.

- **Do not stare passively at commercials.** Discuss their content and the product with children and with one another.

- **Practice turning off the television, the computer, the iPhone, and the iPad.** Explain to your children why you are doing so. Let them see that when things offend or when behavior is becoming addictive, it is wise to exercise such self-control.

In conclusion, Psalm 101:2-3 seems most appropriate:
I will give heed to the blameless way. ...
I will walk within my house in the integrity of my heart.
I will set no worthless thing before my eyes;
I hate the work of those who fall away;
It shall not fasten its grip on me.

## Christianity and the Arts

Many evangelicals have a vague discomfort about the arts. They often are not certain whether art has any meaningful value and are confused about where it fits into God's priorities. Such confusion results in simplistic judgments about art's value in general. This confusion and misunderstanding further result in one of two attitudes about art: antagonism or neglect. Gordon Jackson observes, "Whether by the activism of hostility and antagonism . . . or by the passivity of inaction and neglect, the outcome is the same: There is within evangelical circles minimal patronage of the arts, and even less interest in integrating that segment of culture with the Christian faith." Cultural illiteracy, Jackson argues, is one result; little production of quality art by evangelical Christians is another. For example, writing in 1976, he noted that out of an estimated 33 million church-going evangelicals in the United States, "not even one outstanding novelist has emerged." [17]

## The Value of Art

Dorothy Sayers notes that the very first thing we learn about God is that He creates. [18] Indeed, as the creator of the universe, God is the ultimate example of creative expression:

> If from this world around us we can learn anything about God's character, surely it is that we have a creative God, a God of diversity, a God whose interest in beauty and detail must be unquestioned when one looks at the world which he has made around us, and people themselves as the result of his craftsmanship. [19]

God did not create only for its usefulness, for our enjoyment, or even as a means of revealing His character. Some aspects of His creation are beautiful exhibitions of His creativity and yet never seen by humans. Philip Yancey, in his book *I Was Just Wondering*, asks the question, "Why is it that the most beautiful animals on earth are hidden away from all humans except those wearing SCUBA equipment? Who are they beautiful for?" [20] Evidently, their beauty is for God alone. Schaeffer remarks, "We live in a world full of 'useless' beauty." [21] Therefore, art and beauty have intrinsic value.

As this chapter has already noted, the doctrine of humans as God's image-bearers "takes us deep into the nature of our human creative ability. For one of the marks of the image of God that we bear is that we, too, in our creaturely way, are makers. And in no human activity is this aspect of God's image more evident than in our making art." [22] Just as God's artwork needs no utilitarian justification, neither does ours; it has inherent value because it is given by God as part of His image. It is inherently good in His eyes.

A basic function of art is that it both expresses and shapes people's values and their worldview. [23] This is obvious because art usually deals with the major issues of life: life and death, love and hate, etc. The worldview expressed in a culture's art reflects the worldview of that culture's people. Witness the impact of modern music and entertainment. That is why withdrawal from the arts is so potentially devastating for Christianity. Schaeffer contends, "Any group that willingly or unconsciously sidesteps creativity and human expression gives up their effective role in the society in which they live. In Christian terms, their ability to be the salt of that society is greatly diminished."[24]

A related but slightly different value for artistic expression is that it offers insight into reality. Artistic expression communicates the familiar in a fresh, enlightening way. Art enables one to experience newfound insights into ourselves, others, and the world around us. For example, reading a well-written story about someone grieving over the death of one's father enables one to understand what it is like to lose a father. A good painting about poverty enriches understanding of what it means to be poor.

Art likewise has emotional power. It is able to communicate one perspective of truth as nothing else can. For example, one of the best expressions of God's glory is Handel's *Messiah*. It communicates that subjective element of truth—God's glory—powerfully and unforgettably.

## The Value of Specific Art

Artists create and the diversity of literature, music, dance, cinema, and graphic arts is the result. Within these widely different fields, each piece of art is unique and demands its own critique. If art in general is inherently valuable, is every artwork inherently valuable? Are all artworks equally valuable, or should their value be determined relative to certain standards?

Although human creative ability is part of bearing God's image, this image was marred through the fall into sin. Gaebelein reminds us, "No biblical thinker, whether in aesthetics or in any other field, can afford to slight the fact that, because of the fall, man has an innate bent toward sin, and that bent is reflected in what he does."[25]

As one looks at the art produced in our culture today, much of it is in the realm of good as well as evil—ugliness instead of beauty, falsehood instead of truth. Can such art really have inherent value, really be of inherent good in God's sight? If art has a great potential for good, it also has a great potential for evil. As products of fallen humanity, art is tainted by human sin. As products of finite beings, art is an imperfect expression of the creative nature of God. What then should we do? What criteria should Christians use in evaluating art?

Allow me to suggest three basic criteria for evaluating art and beauty. First, is the artist skilled (i.e., has mastered the artistic medium)? Second, what is the content of the artwork? What is the artist attempting to convey? Is it truth or falsehood? What ethical standards are reflected? What is the worldview? Finally, how creative is the artwork? Does it provide fresh perspective? Does it speak profoundly to the viewer?

In each of the three criteria, God has an ideal for artistic beauty. In skill, He is pleased with excellence; in content, He is pleased with truth; in creativity, He is pleased with quality and depth. Each of these criteria is a reflection of His character—excellence, truth, and creativity. Without trying to oversimplify this complex issue, it seems that the closer a piece of art is to these ideals, the more pleasing it is to God. But beauty remains nebulous, argues Gaebelein:

> ...to justify beauty exclusively with harmony and orderliness does scant justice to the power and truth the arts are capable of....Dissonance in music, stark realism in literature, and the "ugly" in visual art all have an indispensable relation to beauty. The concept of beauty in art must be large enough to include the aesthetic astringencies. For beauty wears different faces.[26]

To be a Christian is not to be taken out of the world and made a purely "spiritual" being. Rather, it is to be transformed into the image God had for humans at creation. Sanctification is the making of real humans. (See 1 Thessalonians 5:23, where the whole "spirit and soul and body" are spoken of in relation to sanctification.) Rookmaaker argues that "...God is the God of life and...the Bible teaches people how to live, how to deal with our world, God's creation."[27] This certainly gives focus to the need for a biblical view of art. Such a focus is reflected in Calvin Seerveld's call for the church to recognize the value and necessity of art:

> This is my argument to you Christians: Given the contemporary situation of clenched despair and practical madness... how can you live openly in this world, God's cosmic theater of wonder, while the (common) graciously preserved unbelievers revel in music and drama, paintings, poetry and dance, with a riot of color, a deafening sound raised in praise to themselves and their false gods, how can you live openly and be silent? ...

That men of darkened understanding can make merry under God's nose and curse him with desperately, damnable forceful art should hurt you ... only different art, not censorship, will take this antithesis earnestly and meet it. [28]

## For Further Discussion

1. How does the author define "creativity"? Do you agree? Offer your own definition.

2. List and elaborate upon the biblical principles of creativity. Cite some examples of each.

3. Comment on the author's contention that the "screen" is an enemy of creativity. Is he calling for the banning of TV, computers, or iPads from Christian homes? Do you agree with his analysis?

4. The author cites several biblical principles for making wise entertainment choices. List and summarize each. Do you agree with them all?

5. The author also lists several practical guidelines for making wise entertainment decisions. List them. Do you agree? Can you add any of your own?

6. The author argues that Christians are often confused about the role of art in their lives. This causes them to either treat art with antagonism or neglect. Explain what he means.

7. The author argues that art has intrinsic value and worth, not only utilitarian value. What does he mean?

8. The author also argues that art serves three additional purposes. Summarize the meaning of each:

   • Art reflects a people's worldview

   • Art reflects reality

   • Art has emotional power

9. The author concludes the chapter by listing three criteria for art that pleases God. What are those three criteria? Explain each.

10. Explain the author's use of Seerveld's quote at the end of the chapter.

## Notes

[1] Andy Crouch, *Culture Making: Recovering Our Creative Calling* (Downers Grove, IL: InterVarsity, 2008), 17-36.

[2] Peter Angeles, *Dictionary of Philosophy* (New York: Barnes & Noble, 1981), 51.

[3] These principles are deduced from a seminar, titled "Creativity in Ministry," presented on the campus of Grace University in the summer of 1992 by Howard Hendricks of Dallas Theological Seminary. Also see Arthur Holmes, *Contours of a World View* (Grand Rapids, MI: Eerdmans, 1983), 206-210.

[4] Richard Zoglin, "Is TV Ruining Our Children?" *Time*, June 19, 1989, 75.

[5] Ibid.

[6] Clement C. Walchshauser, "TV—The Mass Hypnotic," *Fundamentalist Journal*, October 1984, 12.

[7] Linda Winder, "TV: What It's Doing to Your Children," *Living Today*, March–May 1987, 5.

[8] Quentin Schultze, *Television: Manna from Hollywood?* (Grand Rapids, MI: Zondervan, 1986), 150.

[9] Benedict Carey, "TV Limits for Children Urged by American Academy of Pediatrics," *New York Times (New York, NY)*, October 21, 2011.

[10] Ibid. See also Albert Mohler, "The Hypersocialized Generation," www.AlbertMohler.com (blog), June 17 2010, http://www.albertmohler.com/2010/06/17/the-hypersocialized-generation-2/.

[11] Albert Mohler, "After the Revolution," *Tabletalk*, June 2010, 70-71.

[12] Mohler, "The Hypersocialized Generation," (blog).

[13] Matt Richtel, "Digital Devices Deprive Brain of Needed Downtime," *New York Times* (New York, NY), August 24, 2010. Also see his additional articles on this subject in the same publication on August 16, 2010 and June 7, 2010.

[14] Mohler, "The Hypersocialized Generation," (blog).

[15] Ed Stetzer, "The Blessings of the New Media," *Tabletalk*, June 2010, 76-77.

[16] Ibid., 77.

[17] Gordon Jackson, "Evangelicals and the Arts: Divorce or Reconciliation?" *Spectrum*, Summer 1976, 17-19.

[18] Quoted in Frank E. Gaebelein, "Toward a Biblical View of Aesthetics," *Christianity Today*, August 30, 1968, 5.

[19] Francis Schaeffer, *Art and the Bible* (Downers Grove, IL: InterVarsity, 1974), 17.

[20] Philip Yancey, *I Was Just Wondering* (Grand Rapids, MI: Eerdmans, 1989), 3.

[21] Schaeffer, 17.

[22] Gaebelein, 5.

[23] H. R. Rookmaaker, *Art Needs No Justification* (Downers Grove, IL: InterVarsity,

[24] Schaeffer, 24.

[25] Gaebelein, 5.

[26] Ibid., 13.

[27] Rookmaaker, 18.

[28] Calvin Seerveld, *A Christian Critique of Art and Literature* (Toronto: The Association for the Advancement of Christian Scholarship, 1968), 28-29.

# The Christian and
# the Environment
# 12

One of my favorite writers is Andree Seu, who writes for the magazine *World*. In one of her columns, she wrote of reading through a bird magazine she bought at a local PetSmart store. One article particularly in this magazine caused her to write of the author:

> ...by the end of her remarks I felt just a little bit ashamed of being human. It's hard to put your finger on a tone of voice, but here is a sampler: "We love our avian family members and know they love us. Unfortunately, we often hinder the development of a deeper and more precious relationship with them because of how we have been trained to think of animals...[A]s humans we are hindered by our egocentric tendency toward assessing intelligence by how much an animal thinks or behaves as we do... Their ability to adapt to our world is usually far superior to our ability to function in theirs...The animal world...possesses a state of sophistication that is inconceivable and unattainable to most human beings, yet we like to hold ourselves above it."[1]

After reading this, I too felt almost guilty that I am a human being. Perhaps C. S. Lewis provides an antidote to our perceived guilt: He observes that the problem is not that we love animals too much, but that we love God and other human beings too little. In *The Four Loves* he wrote: "It is the smallness of our love for God, not the greatness of our love for the many that constitutes the inordinacy."[2] There is a clear creation-order distinction in the Bible. Humans are created in God's image, not cats. Jesus declared that humans are worth more than birds, even though God cares for both (Matthew 6:26). Further, humans are the ones whom God declares are 'a little lower than the angels (Psalm 8:5, KJV), not dogs.

As we begin thinking Christianly about the relationship between humans, animals, and the environment, we are confronted with a culture that has no ethical foundation to define this relationship. There is, therefore, confusion and sloppy and inconsistent thinking on the subject. For example, this confusion extends even to theology. In 1993, Ron Sider reported that at a 1990 meeting of the World Council of Churches held in Seoul, South Korea, he could not persuade the delegates to add to a resolution on the environment to a statement that read, "We accept the biblical teaching that people alone have been created in the image of God." The debate centered on the term "alone." The majority of attendees at this international conference were unwilling to affirm what historical, biblical theology has always affirmed: Human beings alone are created in the image of God.[3]

Confused thinking about the environment permeates American culture as well. The Hollywood actress Shirley MacLaine (a New Age pantheist) argues that we must begin our thinking with the proposition that we are all gods. Disciplined but unchastened Catholic theologian Matthew Fox says we should turn from a theology centered on sin and redemption and develop a "creation spirituality," with nature as our primary revelation and sin as a distant memory. As far back as 1967, the historian Lynn White, Jr., argued that it is precisely the Christian view of humans as image-bearers and nature as the servant of image-bearers that created our current ecological mess. In effect, he boldly blamed Christianity for the environmental crisis of the modern era. Meanwhile, many evangelicals come close to celebrating the demise of planet earth, enthusiastically citing the decay as proof Christ's return.[4]

Complicating things further is the emergence, within Christianity, of the doctrine of Gaia, most famously represented in Rosemary Ruether's book *Gaia and God: An Ecofeminist Theology of Earth Healing*. Ruether argues that male domination of women and male domination of nature are interconnected. She defines "sin" as wrong relationships among human beings and between them and the rest of nature that foster not just economic and political injustice, along with racism and sexism, but also the destruction of the entire created order. The Gaia hypothesis, so central to Ruether's argument, centers on the thesis that the earth is a living creature. The theory, in fact, imputes a kind of divine power to the earth. "She" is alive and respect for her is at the center of restoring the right relationships destroyed by male dominion.

What are we to think about all of this confused thinking? Is Christianity to blame for the environmental crisis? As Christians, how are we to treat the physical world? What is the value of nonhuman life? How much care do we as Christians need to take in relation to nature? How does God look at nonhuman creation? This was especially brought home to me about seventeen years ago when my daughter, then about age six, was outside systematically killing ants on the sidewalk in front of our home. I asked her what she was doing. She responded, "Daddy, mommy does not like ants, so I am killing them." Sensing that this was a teachable moment, I asked her, "Joanna, do you think God is pleased with killing ants like this? Are they in mommy's cupboards? Are they hurting us here on the walk?" She did not know how to respond at first. Our subsequent talk focused on treating God's creatures with respect because God holds us accountable for managing His creation well. I doubt she understood all we discussed, but it began a process of teaching her about the stewardship of God's creation.

In 1970, long before most evangelical Christians were even thinking about the environment, Francis Schaeffer published one of his most important books, *Pollution and the Death of Man: The Christian View of Ecology*. It remains a pioneering work and continues to influence my thinking on the environment and my responsibility to God in this area. Schaeffer asked the right questions and proposed answers centered on Scripture and biblical theology. Although more than forty years old, Schaeffer's book continues to be a relevant starting point for constructing a biblical view of the environment, which is evident from this chapter.

## Inadequate Views on Human Responsibility toward Creation

Theology is the proper place to begin thinking about how we are to view the physical environment. There are at least three inadequate theological perspectives in the culture today. First is the Christian view, often associated with St. Francis of Assisi, that all aspects of God's physical creation are equal, that there is, for example, no difference between the birds and humans. Legends about Francis have him preaching to the birds and giving counsel to a wolf threatening a small town in Italy. Francis is often associated with the environmental movement, with his statue prominent in environmental literature and promotional material. But the particulars of God's creation are not equal. Genesis 1 and 2 make it clear that humans are the crown of God's creation. Humans are the only ones who bear His image. In terms of God's redemptive plan, Jesus did not die for birds; He died for human beings.

Second is pantheism, the view that all reality is one: All is God and God is all. With the growth of postmodern pluralism and the increasing appeal of Eastern worldviews (e.g., Hinduism and Buddhism), pantheism is a growing and attractive worldview. Its influence on the environmental movement is significant. For example, the reason we should not cut down California Redwoods is because they are god. The reason we save the whales is because they are god. Such is the pantheistic position reflected in the views of Shirley MacLaine, the Gaia hypothesis, and the entire New Age worldview. But the Bible will have none of this. The Bible does teach the immanence of God—that He is present everywhere (e.g., Psalm 139), but it rejects the teaching that all is God. He created all things and yet is above and beyond His physical creation (the biblical doctrine of God's transcendence). The Bible insists that we keep God's immanence and His transcendence in balance, for both are true. God is personal, yet sovereign; He is immanent, yet transcendent. Therefore, for biblical Christianity, pantheism is simply an unacceptable position.

Third is a commitment to a platonic dichotomy, i.e., that the spiritual world is all that is important; the material world has no value to God or to us as His disciples. The world is passing away so it does not matter whether we treat it well or abuse it. The Bible will have none of this either. Scripture details the goodness of God's creation (e.g., Genesis 1 and 2; 1 Timothy 4:4). It is simply wrong to reject God's physical creation as evil. Furthermore, the physical body is of such importance to God that He will one day resurrect it. Nothing speaks more powerfully about its goodness than that. Further, the physical world, still under the curse because of human sin (see Genesis 3), is still central to God's ultimate redemptive plan. Indeed, Isaiah 65 and Revelation 21–22 speak powerfully of a new heaven and new earth, when the physical world will be restored to its original perfection and glory (also see Romans 8). Any type of dualistic worldview that declares the physical world is evil and only the spirit world is good is false and must be rejected.

## A Word about Climate Change

That the climate of planet earth, especially its warming, is changing is a given. The exact cause of this change is not certain. For the most part, the world has only been keeping reliable records concerning climate, temperature, and other metrological data since about 1895. As many of my meteorological friends have remarked, we simply do not have a great deal of reliable data to fully understand the cycles of climate change, temperature variation, and weather patterns. But, because we as Christians are to be good stewards of God's world, we simply must do all we can to understand this phenomenon. To that end, Robert Bryce of the Manhattan Institute has written a most helpful article titled, "Five Truths about Climate Change."[5] Because there is so much hype and emotional baggage surrounding this topic, it is always refreshing when you read something that is balanced and insightful. Bryce acknowledges the reality of a global change in temperatures but, in doing so, he presents factual data and observations that place an issue such as this in a helpful perspective. Here is a summary of his argument:

- **Carbon-dioxide emissions have been the environmental issue of the early 21st century.** For example, former Vice President Al Gore has relentlessly focused during this past decade on carbon emissions as the singular most important cause of the increase in global temperatures. The Intergovernmental Panel on Climate Change has basically agreed. Worldwide there was talk of a global tax or placing limits on carbon dioxide emissions. There were promises, for example, from the world community when it gathered in Copenhagen in 2009, but there was no decisive action on either a tax or limits on carbon dioxide. So, during this past decade, carbon emissions rose by 28 percent. As Bryce observes, "Those increases reflect soaring demand for electricity, up by 36 percent, which in turn fostered a 47 percent increase in coal consumption. (Natural gas use increased by 29 percent while oil use grew by 13 percent.) Carbon-dioxide emissions are growing because people around the world understand the essentiality of electricity to modernity. And for many countries, the cheapest way to produce electricity is by burning coal."

- **Regardless of the cause of the global increase in temperatures, the world simply must produce a great deal more energy to remain productive and comfortable.** And right now the vast majority of that energy need comes from hydrocarbons.

- **The carbon dioxide issue is not about the United States anymore.** During the past decade, carbon dioxide emissions in the United States fell by 1.7 percent, and, according to the International Energy Agency, the United States is now cutting carbon emissions faster than Europe, even though the European Union has instituted an elaborate carbon-trading, pricing scheme. Simply put, the United States is producing vast quantities of cheap natural gas from shale, which is displacing higher-carbon coal. In contrast, China's carbon emissions jumped by 123 percent over the past decade, surpassing the United States by more than 2 billion tons per year. Africa's carbon dioxide emissions jumped by 40 percent, Asia's by 44 percent and the Middle East's by 57 percent! Thus, even if you omitted the United States from all carbon emissions usage, the use of carbon worldwide would have gone up.

- **The world must become more efficient in its energy production—and it is.** Today's best natural gas fired turbines have thermal efficiencies of 60 percent (compared with the original turbines of Thomas Edison, which converted less than 3 percent of the heat energy of the coal being burned into electricity). Bryce argues that "nearly all of the things we use on a daily basis—light bulbs, computers, automobiles—are vastly more efficient that they were just a few years ago."

- **If we accept the proposition that carbon emissions are bad, it is not really that clear exactly what we should do about this.** For example, Tom Wigley of the National Center for Atmospheric Research in Boulder recently published a report that determined "switching from coal to natural gas would do little for the global climate." Wigley discovered that particulates put into the atmosphere by coal-fired power plants, "although detrimental to the environment, cool the planet by blocking incoming sunlight." Thus, using energy sources that emit no particulates, like nuclear or natural gas, will not make a major difference in averting near-term changes in the climate caused by carbon dioxide. It also follows that widespread use of renewable energy (e.g., wind and solar energy) will not make a difference either. The bottom line of much of this discussion is that those who are so critical of carbon emissions really have no credible alternatives to replace the hydrocarbons that now provide 87 percent of the world's energy.

Every now and then, we must step back and ascertain what the truth is about climate change and carbon emissions. Robert Bryce has done so in his essay. Our world is dependent on hydrocarbons for its energy sources. There is nothing currently on the horizon that will alter this simple fact.

## The Church and Love for Animals: Is It Biblical?

Christine Gutleben, the Humane Society's first director of faith outreach, has stated that "animal ministries are in every state, and they do everything, including pet food in traditional food drives, to donating to local shelters, designating church grounds as animal sanctuaries, hosting adoption events, printing animals for adoption in church bulletins." She also reveals that many churches include pets in their antipoverty work: "They will host an event for the surrounding community, and provide medical and dental care for people, but also have a veterinarian who will provide free vaccines on church grounds." In St. Louis, there is a pet ministry, which is a part of Grace Church, a large non-denominational Protestant congregation, called Noah's Ark. It runs a pet-food drive, supports no-kill rescue of animals, brings pets to visit the sick and infirm, and hosts a grief group for those who have lost a pet. The Church of the King in New Orleans holds monthly events for pets, and when they do, hundreds of people line up for their pets to get vaccines. Indeed, Laura Hobgood-Oster, of Southwestern University in Georgetown, Texas, and the author of *Holy Dogs and Asses: Animals in the History of the Christian Tradition,* argues, "Animals have always been central to Christianity, as well as all the world's major religions." Further, many Roman Catholics are taught that St. Francis of Assisi communed with the birds and spoke with a wolf; thus, on his feast day, October 4, many churches host events in which animals are blessed by a priest or other church officials.[6]

How should we think about such developments within the broader Christian church? Is this a biblical response to our stewardship responsibility as dominion stewards of God's world? How should we think biblically about our pets? It is time now to focus on several biblical principles to aid Christian believers in thinking about animal life, the larger physical world, and our relationship to both.

## Biblical Principles for a Proper View of the Environment

First, **a proper biblical view of the physical creation begins with a proper view of God.** The challenge is to keep in balance God's transcendence and His immanence. God's transcendence focuses on His radical separateness from creation; He is both above and beyond His physical world. God's immanence focuses on His presence in His physical world. To stress His immanence at the expense of His transcendence is to land in pantheism where everything is god. To stress His transcendence at the expense of His immanence is to see the physical world as insignificant and a tool for exploitation. Neither is satisfactory nor God-honoring. In our theology, there must be a balance between both God's transcendence and His immanence, between His intimate involvement with all aspects of His physical creation (see Psalm 139) and His radical distinction from creation. Where it is finite, limited, dependent, He is infinite, unlimited and self-sufficient.[7]

Second, is **a proper view of human beings.** Human beings are both interdependent with the rest of creation and unique within it, because we alone bear His image and have stewardship responsibility over the earth. Christians frequently forget our interdependence with the rest of God's world. Our daily existence depends on water, sun and air. There is indeed a global ecosystem.[8] It matters how we treat the water, the trees and the other animals. If they are harmed, so are we. There is this vital, interdependent relationship that comes from the creative hand of God.

But the Bible also declares human uniqueness. This book has made much of humans as image-bearers of God. No other physical part of God's world can claim this. Humans also have dominion status. God declares in Genesis 1:26-30 that humans have the responsibility to rule (have dominion) over the nonhuman creation. Tragically, this dominion has frequently turned to exploitation. As argued in chapter ten of this book, Genesis 2:15 is the corrective to exploitation. Humans are to serve and watch lovingly, almost worshipfully, over God's creation. We are God's stewards over His creation. He has the sovereignty; we have the dominion.

Francis Schaeffer also argues that humans have two relationships—one upward and one downward. The upward relationship accentuates the personal relationship humans can have, through salvation, with God—a relationship not enjoyed by the rest of the created order. The downward relationship accentuates the "creaturely" relationship that humans share with the rest of the created order (see Genesis 2:7; Job 34:14-15). As with most issues, the struggle is to keep the two in balance. We tend to so highlight the upward relationship to the virtual exclusion of the downward. This leads to horrific neglect or ruthless exploitation of the physical world. Or we tend to highlight the downward to the virtual exclusion of the upward. This is the gross error of the evolutionary hypothesis, which sees humans as the product of the impersonal force of natural selection, not of God's purposeful design. [9]

Third, **the nonhuman creation is of great significance to God.** He created the physical world as a deliberate act. God also takes pleasure in His physical world. This is clear from the Creation Ordinance in Genesis 1 and 2 and from 1 Timothy 4:4: "For everything created by God is good, and nothing is to be rejected if it is received with gratitude." (See also Psalm 104:31 where we see God rejoicing in His works.) The point is that if the physical world is of importance to God, then it must be to us—His creatures—as well (see also Job 39:1-2; Colossians 1:16; Psalm 19:1-4).

As Ron Sider points out, it is likewise imperative to note that God has a covenant, not only with humans, but also with the nonhuman creation. After the flood, God made a covenant with the physical creation: "Now behold, I Myself do establish My covenant with you, and with your descendants after you; and with every living creature that is with you, the birds, the cattle, and every beast of the earth with you; of all that comes out of the ark, even every beast of the earth" (Genesis 9:9-10). The physical world has dignity, worth and value quite apart from its service to humanity.

Incredibly, God's redemptive plan has a cosmic quality to it. As Sider states, "This fact provides a crucial foundation for building a Christian theology for an environmental age." [10] The biblical hope that the whole created order, including the material world of bodies and rivers and trees, will be part of the kingdom confirms that the created order is good and important. Romans 8:19-23 demonstrates that at Christ's return, the groaning of creation will cease, for the creation will be transformed: "The creation itself will be liberated from its bondage to decay and brought into the glorious freedom of the children of God" (v. 21, NIV).

## The Motivation for Good Stewardship

Since we are God's stewards over His creation, what should be our motivation? Are we good stewards for pragmatic reasons or for moral reasons? The pragmatic view posits that we should be good stewards over God's world because our very survival depends on it. For example, if we farm the hills irresponsibly, we will lose topsoil and harm our ability to produce food. If we wantonly kill snakes, eventually we will be overrun by rodents. If we mine copper irresponsibly, we will cause horrendous erosion that harms the water. If we burn the rainforests, we pollute the air and destroy oxygen-producing trees, which in turn threaten our supply of oxyGenesis But the Bible rejects this as the sole motivating force for good stewardship.

Instead, Scripture implores humans to exercise good stewardship over the physical world because to do so demonstrates honor and respect for God's created order. The physical creation should not be exploited because it is morally wrong to misuse God's created order. Having God's perspective, we responsibly farm, we shun wanton destruction of animal life, we responsibly mine copper, and we cease recklessly burning the rainforests because we respect and honor that which God has honored and respected. We show honor to the physical world with which God has a covenant relationship. Christians should, therefore, be the leaders in responsible environmentalism. As God's theocratic stewards, we represent Him when we honor His physical world.

## The Environmental Solution

Schaeffer argues that the church needs to be a "pilot plant" where the proper relationships between human beings and the physical world are modeled. [11] The church, he states, must be a place "where men can see in our congregations and missions a substantial healing of all divisions, the alienations, man's rebellion has produced." [12] This macro-plan for reconciliation must begin with the church. It involves five dimensions:

- **Humans properly related to God.** For any type of reconciliation to occur, humans must trust Jesus Christ for salvation. This is what the Apostle Paul meant when he referred to his ministry as one of "reconciliation" (2 Corinthians 5:18)—reconciling God and humanity through the finished work of Jesus Christ. Humans will never exercise proper God-honoring stewardship without first being reconciled to Him through Christ.

- **The human properly related to self.** Humans must see themselves as God sees them—of infinite value as creatures and, in Christ, as redeemed. Because we have God's view of self, there is proper respect for the body as eternally significant. A mark of the redeemed Christian is a commitment to care for and respect one's body. It belongs to God, and to allow it to be an instrument of sin or to treat it with disrespect is to say something about God, for He created and redeemed it. The Christian is no longer autonomous but forever dependent on the Lord (see Romans 12:1-2; 1 Corinthians 6:19-20).

- **Humans properly related to other humans.** Because we now have Christ's mind (1 Corinthians 2:16), Christians also view other humans through God's eyes. Christians treat all humans with respect, realizing shared creatureliness and shared value as image-bearers of God. This is at the heart of Jesus' command to love God with heart, soul, mind, and strength and our neighbors as ourselves. The Good Samaritan story powerfully illustrates how one loves one's neighbor (Luke 10:30-37). All humans, redeemed and unredeemed, are of value and worth to God.

- **Humans properly related to nature.** Humans are to treat all aspects of God's physical creation with respect and honor. If all of God's creation is "good," then His disciples must have the same regard He has. It is ethically wrong to destroy wantonly what God has created. The nonhuman creation serves humanity, which is the point of having dominion status. But humans serve God's creation with respect and honor; we are God's stewards representing Him. Stewardship also implies accountability—to Him.

- **Nature properly related to nature.** Remarkably, Romans 8:20-23 highlights the present "groaning" of creation; it awaits the return of Jesus when it will be restored to its glory and its productivity. Then nature will be properly related to nature and the horrific consequences of human sin that so wreak havoc on the physical creation (see Genesis 3) will end. Nature's destiny is the new heaven and new earth detailed in Isaiah 65 and Revelation 21–22.

In 1988, Mother Teresa and James Lovelock, advocate of the Gaia hypothesis, engaged in a heated debate at Oxford University's Global Forum for Survival. Mother Teresa argued that if we take care of people on the planet, the earth will survive. Lovelock countered that if we take care of the earth, humanity's problems will be solved. [13] In light of God's Word, both are needed. God makes it clear that if there is repentance and cleansing, He will cleanse the earth as well (see 2 Chronicles 7:14, for example). As Christian stewards of God's world, there is the crying need to care for both humans and the earth, for both are important to God.

Christians must be at the forefront of the environmental movement so that God's glory is not preempted by a narrow humanistic agenda nor an "antihuman" value system endemic to modern pantheism. We must not conclude that the earth is good and humanity evil. Also, we must not conclude that being concerned about the environment makes one an advocate of some form of pantheism or the Gaia hypothesis. The beauty and complexity of the earth are God's good gifts and we must cultivate respect and honor for God's physical creation. We are His stewards and He is watching!

### For Further Discussion

1. In the chapter's introduction, the author cites several wrong views about the relationship between humans and the physical environment. What is the Gaia hypothesis?

2. There are several inadequate views about the environment. Explain each of the following:

   • St. Francis of Assisi

   • Pantheism

   • Platonic Dichotomy

3. The author details three biblical principles for understanding God's perspective on the environment. Explain each of the following:

   • A proper view of God

   • A proper view of humans

   • A proper view of nature

4. Motivation on proper stewardship of the environment is critical. What is the difference between a pragmatic motivation and a moral motivation? Explain.

5. Relying on Francis Schaeffer, the author proposes an "environmental solution" that consists of five levels. Explain each level:

   • Humans properly related to God

   • Humans having a proper view of self

- Humans properly related to other humans
- Humans properly related to nature
- Nature properly related to nature

# Notes

[1] Andree Seu, *World*, January 28, 2012, 71.

[2] C. S. Lewis, *The Four Loves* (New York: Harcourt, Brace, Jovanovich, 1960), 25-39.

[3] Ronald J. Sider, "Redeeming the Environmentalists," *Christianity Today*, June 21 1993, 26.

[4] Ibid.

[5] Robert Bryce, "Five Truths about Climate Change," *Wall Street Journal* (New York, NY), October 6, 2011.

[6] Mark Oppenheimer, "Pet Ministries Are Growing in Churches," *New York Times* (New York, NY), October 15, 2011.

[7] Sider, 28.

[8] Ibid.

[9] Francis A. Schaeffer, *Pollution and the Death of Man: The Christian View of Ecology* (Wheaton, IL: Tyndale, 1970), 47-61.

[10] Sider, 29.

[11] Schaeffer, 81-93.

[12] Ibid., 82.

[13] Tod Connor, "Is the Earth Alive?" *Christianity Today*, January 11, 1993, 25.

# Bibliography

Angeles, Peter. *Dictionary of Philosophy.* New York: Barnes & Noble, 1981.

Baker, Don. *Beyond Rejection.* Portland: Multnomah, 1985.

Berkouwer, G. C. *Man: Image of God.* Grand Rapids, MI: Eerdmans, 1962.

Bernabaum, John A., and Simon A. Steer. *Why Work?* Grand Rapids, MI: Baker, 1986.

Colson, Charles. *Kingdoms in Conflict.* Grand Rapids, MI: Zondervan, 1987.

Craigie, Peter. *The Problem of War in the Old Testament.* Grand Rapids, MI: Zondervan, 1978.

Cramer, Stanley, and Edwin L. Herr. *Career Guidance and Counseling Through the Life Span.* Boston: Little Brown, 1979.

Crouch, Andy. *Culture Making: Recovering Our Creative Calling.* Downers Grove, IL: InterVarsity, 2008.

Crouse, Bill. *Abortion and Human Value.* Dallas: Probe, 1979.

Eidsmoe, John. *God and Caesar.* Wheaton, IL: Crossway, 1989.

Feinberg, Joel, ed. *The Problem of Abortion.* Nashville: Belmont, 1973.

Feinberg, John, and Paul Feinberg. *Ethics for a Brave New World.* Wheaton, IL: Crossway, 1993.

Fletcher, Joseph. *Situation Ethics.* Philadelphia: Westminster, 1966.

Geisler, Norman. *Christian Ethics: Options and Issues.* Grand Rapids, MI: Baker, 1989.

George, Robert P., and Christopher Tollefsen. *Embryo: A Defense of Human Life.* New York: Doubleday, 2008.

Hoekema, Anthony. *Created in God's Image.* Grand Rapids, MI: Eerdmans, 1986.

Holmes, Arthur. *Contours of a World View.* Grand Rapids, MI: Eerdmans, 1983.

Hutchcraft, Ron. *The Battle for a Generation.* Chicago: Moody Press, 1996.

Lewis, C. S. *The Four Loves.* New York: Harcourt, Brace, Jovanovich, 1960.

Luce, Ron. *Battle Cry for a Generation: The Fight to Save America's Youth.* Colorado Springs: Cook Communications Ministries, 2005.

Lutzer, Erwin. *The Necessity of Ethical Absolutes.* Dallas: Probe, 1981.

Meilander, Gilbert. *Neither Beast Nor God: The Dignity of the Human Person.* New York: New Atlantis Books, 2009.

Moore, Keith L., and T. V. N. Persaud. *The Developing Human: Clinically Oriented Embryology.* 6th ed. Philadelphia: W. B. Saunders Company, 1998.

Piper, John, and Wayne Grudem. *Recovering Biblical Manhood and Womanhood.* Wheaton, IL: Crossway, 1991.

Pojman, Louis P. *Ethics: Discovering Right and Wrong.* Belmont, CA: Wadsworth, 1995.

Rookmaaker, H. R. *Art Needs No Justification.* Downers Grove, IL: InterVarsity, 1978.

Ross, Alan, Jr. *Creation and Blessing.* Grand Rapids, MI: Baker, 1988.

Ryrie, Charles. *You Mean the Bible Teaches That . . .* Chicago: Moody Press, 1974.

Sandel, Michael. *The Case Against Perfection: Ethics in the Age of Genetic Engineering.* Boston: Belknap Press, 2007.

Satinover, Jeffrey. *Homosexuality and the Politics of Truth.* Grand Rapids, MI: Baker, 1996.

Schaeffer, Francis. *Art and the Bible.* Downers Grove, IL: InterVarsity, 1974.

———. *How Should We Then Live?* Old Tappan, NJ: Revell, 1976.

———. *Pollution and the Death of Man: The Christian View of Ecology.* Wheaton, IL: Tyndale, 1970.

Schaeffer, Francis, and C. Everett Koop. *Whatever Happened to the Human Race?* Old Tappan, NJ: Revell, 1979.

Schaeffer, Franky. *Addicted to Mediocrity: Contemporary Christians and the Arts.* Westchester, IL: Cornerstone, 1981.

Schultze, Quentin. *Television: Manna from Hollywood?* Grand Rapids, MI: Zondervan, 1986.

Seerveld, Calvin. *A Christian Critique of Art and Literature.* Toronto: The Association for the Advancement of Christian Scholarship, 1968.

Skinner, B. F. *Beyond Freedom and Dignity.* New York: Knopf, 1971.

Sproul, R. C. *Ethics and the Christian.* Wheaton, IL: Tyndale House, 1986.

Stott, John. *Involvements.* Grand Rapids, MI: Zondervan, 1985.

Webber, Robert E. *The Secular Saint: A Case for Evangelical Social Responsibility.* Grand Rapids, MI: Zondervan, 1979.

Wilkie, John. *Handbook on Abortion.* Cincinnati, OH: Hiltz, 1971.

Yancey, Philip. *I Was Just Wondering.* Grand Rapids, MI: Eerdmans, 1989.